Justification by Faith

Zaccheus Studies: New Testament

General Editor: Mary Ann Getty, RSM

Justification by Faith

The Implications of
Romans 3:27-31

by

Jan Lambrecht, S.J., and
Richard W. Thompson

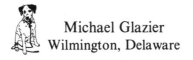
Michael Glazier
Wilmington, Delaware

About the Authors

Jan Lambrecht, S.J., is Professor of New Testament and Biblical Greek at the Catholic University of Leuven in Belgium. His articles have appeared in many scholarly journals and his books include *Once More Astonished: The Parables of Jesus Christ* and *The Sermon on The Mount.*

Richard W. Thompson received his PhD in Religious Studies from the Catholic University of Leuven. He is currently on the biblical staff at St. Francis Seminary in Milwaukee.

First published in 1989 by Michael Glazier, Inc., 1935 West Fourth Street, Wilmington, Delaware 19805.

Library of Congress Cataloging-in-Publication Data

Lambrecht, Jan.
  Justification by faith.

  (Zacchaeus studies. New Testament)
  1. Bible. N.T.   Romans III, 27-31—Criticism, interpretation, etc.   2. Justification—Biblical teaching.   I. Thompson, Richard William.   II. Title.   III. Series.
BS2665.2.L37   1988   227'.106   88-82447
ISBN 0-89453-665-6
ISBN: Zacchaeus Studies, NT: 0-89453-662-1

Cover Design by Maureen Daney
Typography by Edith Warren
Printed in the United States of America by St. Mary's Press

Table of Contents

Editor's Note

Zacchaeus Studies provide concise, readable and relatively inexpensive scholarly studies on particular aspects of scripture and theology. The New Testament section of the series presents studies dealing with focal or debated questions; and the volumes focus on specific texts of particular themes of current interest in biblical interpretation. Specialists have their professional journals and other forums where they discuss matters of mutual concern, exchange ideas and further contemporary trends of research; and some of their work on contemporary biblical research is now made accessible for students and others in *Zacchaeus Studies*.

The authors in this series share their own scholarship in non-technical language, in the areas of their expertise and interest. These writers stand with the best in current biblical scholarship in the English-speaking world. Since most of them are teachers, they are accustomed to presenting difficult material in comprehensible form without compromising a high level of critical judgment and analysis.

The works of this series are ecumenical in content and purpose and cross credal boundaries. They are designed to augment formal and informal biblical study and discussion. Hopefully they will also serve as texts to enhance and supplement seminary, university and college classes. The series will also aid Bible study groups, adult education and parish religious education classes to develop intelligent, versatile and challenging programs for those they serve.

Mary Ann Getty RSM
New Testament Editor

Foreword

The study of such a small unit of text as Romans 3:27-31 might initially appear to be so specialized as to be of interest only to those who are concerned with the finer points of Pauline theology. It might seem that only after study of all of the Pauline letters in general could one benefit from such a close look at such a limited pericope. In reality, however, the unit of text which we examine in this book contains some of the most fundamental themes of Paul's thought, themes that appear not only throughout the entire letter to the Romans, but that also form much of the background of the letter to the Galatians, for example.

One does not need more than a general background in Paul, then, to understand and benefit from the present work. A close look at Romans 3:27-31 can easily introduce the beginning student of Paul to some of his fundamental ideas, and can itself serve as a background for further, more concentrated study.

No doubt most readers who are somewhat familiar with Paul will be aware of his teaching that justification is by faith. The classical text normally used for illustrating this idea can be found in Romans 3:28: "For we hold that a person is justified by faith apart from works of law". Martin Luther translated this verse to say that a person is justified only by faith, *sola fide*, and today, most Protestant and Catholic scholars agree with this understanding, which emphasizes the priority of faith.

Nevertheless, in spite of this long and respected tradition which claims Romans 3:28 as the *locus classicus* for Paul's teaching on justification by faith, the present work does not deal primarily with this fundamental aspect of Paul's thought. Rather, in the course of our study, we shall discover that Paul is using his idea that justification is by faith (which he assumes one already knows and believes) in order to lead his readers to the fundamental consequence that necessarily must follow from this starting point. This consequence, which really forms the essential teaching of the whole unit (Romans 3:27-31) is that, if justif-ication is by faith, then God has revealed that he is truly the God of all men and women. For Paul, this means that God is the God of Jew and Gentile alike. Jews may have a special claim on God based on their past and present relationship with him in the Mosaic covenant, but since "all humans have sinned" (3:23), as far as justification is concerned, "there is no distinction" (3:22) between them and the Gentiles.

The primary focus of Romans 3:27-31, then, is the *universality* of God's redeeming love as it has been revealed in Christ. Paul firmly believes that justification is by faith. But in this section of Romans he is most concerned with showing not simply what justification by faith *is* but what justification by faith, in its ramifications, *means*. And it means an end to that attitude of superiority, of "being better off" (3:9) because of privileged relations with God.

Paul calls this feeling of privilege "boasting," and in Romans 3:27 he flatly announces that it has been excluded, once and for all. The Jews no longer have any right to think that, as Jews, they are any closer to God than anyone else. For just like Gentiles, they are sinners. In 3:27 and 3:28, Paul summarizes major arguments that he has presented earlier in the letter as to why he thinks this boasting has no more place in Jewish life.

In 3:29-30, Paul draws the innovative conclusion that since justification of the sinner is by faith, and boasting in privileged status is thereby eliminated, everyone must now see that God is equally the God of Jew and non-Jew alike. In other words, God's redeeming love for the world is a universal love. God deals with all men and women on one and the same basis, faith. Bluntly put, for Paul, who realizes that every human is in need of justification, being a Jew means almost nothing; having faith in Christ means everything.

We can easily imagine the reaction of those faithful Jews whose lives had been in response to God's covenant with Moses. "You are destroying our law, Paul! You are depriving the law of any real meaning in our lives!" This objection is raised against Paul in 3:31, and he answers it concisely: "On the contrary, we uphold the law."

Paul's claim to uphold the very law that he seems to criticize so heavily is one that many have found to be unconvincing. Even contemporary students of Paul are often unpersuaded by his protestation. We will attempt to show that at least Paul himself was convinced by what he said, and we will look for specific examples of how he upheld the law (and by this we mean the entire law) in parts of Romans 4 and Romans 8.

Finally, at the end of the study, some concluding reflections of contemporary relevance will be offered. Paul's gospel of God's universal love continues to challenge Christians to accept this love; and not only to accept what it means for their self-understanding, but also to live it out in their ordinary lives.

This study of Romans 3:27-31 originated in the doctoral dissertation of Richard W. Thompson for the Catholic University of Louvain, defended in 1985. It was directed by Father Jan Lambrecht, S.J. The mentor-student relationship that was enjoyed by both parties during the course of the work has resulted in this collaboration on the present text. Both authors share equal responsibility for the content.

We are grateful to Michael Glazier Publishers for including the book in their *Zacchaeus Studies*. Further thanks is expressed to Rev. Thomas Brundage, priest of the Archdiocese of Milwaukee, Wisconsin, for his careful reading of the manuscript and his helpful suggestions regarding style. Of course, all responsibility for any imperfections in the work falls to the authors.

Jan Lambrecht, S.J.
Katholieke Universiteit
Leuven, Belgium

Richard W. Thompson
St. Francis Seminary
Milwaukee, Wisconsin

1

Paul's Double Criticism of Jewish Boasting
Romans 3:27

Then what becomes of our boasting? It is excluded.
On what principle? On the principle of works?
No, but on the principle of faith.

Anyone who takes up Paul's letter to the Romans at chap. 3, v 27[1] and attempts to understand the gist of Paul's reasoning there is caught short by the feeling that he or she has plunged into the middle of the discussion. And this is indeed the case. Verse 27 immediately appears to be drawing conclusions from some previous argument, for in that verse, Paul begins with a question: "Then what becomes of our boasting?" The very first word, "then" (in the Greek text this is the second word, *oun*) alerts one to the importance of something that has already been said. It pushes the reader back to points that have already been made, to positions taken, that are now (at v 27) going to be

---

[1] For a more technical presentation of our position on Romans 3:27, see Richard W. Thompson, "Paul's Double Critique of Jewish Boasting: A Study of Rom 3,27 in Its Context," *Biblica* 67 (1986) 520-31, and Jan Lambrecht, "Why is Boasting Excluded? A Note on Rom 3,27 and 4,2," *Ephemerides Theologicae Lovanienses* 61 (1985) 365-69. See also Thompson, "*We Uphold the Law,*" *A Study of Rom 3,31 and Its Context,* Unpubl. Ph.D. Dissertation, Leuven 1985, pp. 193-212.

brought to some sort of conclusion. This word "then" tells the reader that in order to understand this verse, he or she must back up a bit in the letter to get the broader context of the discussion which is now being brought to a conclusion.
of the discussion which is now being brought to a conclusion.

A. The Broader Context of Romans 3:27

The observation just made introduces a question into our discussion. Exactly how far back in the letter are we supposed to go in order to take into account all the material that Paul is now drawing to a conclusion in v 27? The answer to this question is actually suggested in 3:27 itself by the presence of the term "boasting." How are these two data—the "then" pointing backwards and the term "boasting"—related?

First, we must acknowledge that, no doubt, every reader of Romans 3:27 has a spontaneous idea as to what boasting is. When Paul says here that boasting has been excluded, everyone feels that he or she knows what kind of boasting Paul is talking about. Surely it must be related to some sort of pride. Perhaps it refers to bragging, and must be based in a certain feeling of superiority. But if we wish to remain somewhat "objective" interpreters of the text, we must ask whether we can immediately (and so easily) assume that we know what Paul is talking about here. Is there any evidence *in the text* that Paul is here speaking in general terms about a person's sense of self-sufficiency, the almost innate notion that we are all "masters of our fate"? Are we justified in thinking that Paul is talking about a general human trait, a sort of *hybris* which characterizes our endeavors to reach whatever goals we have set for ourselves?

However natural this understanding of boasting may appear to be, we must keep in mind the introductory "then" of our verse. Paul is not *initiating* a discussion about boasting here, but is actually *continuing* a discussion that is already in progress when we join it at 3:27. This opens up the possibility that Paul is not merely drawing on a general notion of boasting but is actually referring to something he has already discussed earlier in the letter. We must ask, therefore, if Paul has already given some clue as to what he means by "boasting." When we start our search for how much of the letter to the Romans forms the background of 3:27 we will see that Romans 3:27 does not represent Paul's first statement about boasting. Paul has already indicated what he means by the term at chap. 2, vv 17-23.

Before studying that passage, however, we can notice how the term "boasting" has helped us answer our first question about the broader context of Romans 3:27. Paul is drawing conclusions in this verse, and in our search for the beginning of his argument (prompted by the introductory "then") we have discovered that the "boasting" he is talking about has already been discussed in 2:17-23. This means that the concluding statement in 3:27 must be understood as a culmination of an argument that has started already at Romans 2:17, the first time Paul talks about boasting. Furthermore, we must now express a certain reservation about our initial and spontaneous understanding of "boasting" in 3:27. The general meaning of "pride" or "accomplishment" that we give to the term may not be what Paul has in mind at all. But in order to decide what boasting means for Paul (as distinct from what it may naturally mean to us), we must first go back to Romans 2:17-23.[2]

---

[2]Although many exegetes in the past have understood boasting in Rom 3:27 as a general human characteristic, the necessity of linking 3:27 with Romans 2:17 (and thus narrowing the concept of boasting) has appeared, for example, in the recent work of René Lafontaine, "Pour une nouvelle évangélization. L'emprise universelle de la justice de Dieu selon l'épître aux Romans 1,18-2,29," *Nouvelle Revue Théologique* 108 (1986) 641-65, pp. 661-62; see also Heikki Räisänen, *Paul and the Law*, Wissenrshaftliche Untersuchungen zum Neuen Testament 29, Tübingen: J.C.B. Mohr, 1983, p. 170; Ed P. Sanders, *Paul, the Law, and the Jewish People*, Philadelphia: Fortress Press, 1983, p. 33; Idem, *Paul and Palestinian Judaism, A Comparison of Patterns of Religion*, London: SCM Press, 1977, p. 550.

B. The Meaning of "Boasting"

In Romans 2:17 we arrive in the midst of another discussion which Paul is carrying on with a Jewish audience. This discussion probably starts at 2:1, and up through v 16 concerns the relationship between a person's behavior (based on following the demands of the law; see vv 6-15) and the future judgment of each individual by God in Jesus Christ (see vv 1-5.16)

In v 17 Paul addresses his Jewish discussion partner by using a threefold description of what being a Jew meant in Paul's day: (1) calling oneself a Jew; (2) relying on the law; and (3) boasting of one's relation to God. Two points are worth noting in this description of Jewish idenity. First, Paul is not the only person to draw a connection between Jewishness, the law, and security in one's relation to God. A number of scholars are agreed that this triad represents a typical example of Jewish self-understanding of the first century (see, for example the Syriac Apocalypse of Baruch 48,22: "In you we have put our trust, because, behold, your Law is with us, and we know that we do not fall as long as we keep your statutes").

This self-understanding includes the idea that to be a Jew meant that one followed the law of Moses, not only the law as it was contained in the Pentateuch, but no doubt the law as it was transmitted and formulated by the scribes (the so called "oral law") as well. This faithful and obedient participation in the Mosaic law, and thereby in God's covenant with Moses, enabled the Jew to enjoy a certain sense of security that he or she stood in a right relation with God, that he or she walked according to the ways of the Lord. This confidence in one's relation to God, a confidence based on following the law of Moses, is here connected with "boasting" (2:17). Surely, if Jews considered themselves good Jews and relied on God's law, they would certainly have reason to boast. Or so they thought.

Second, that Paul draws on a contemporary Jewish understanding of what being a Jew meant shows us that he is probably not presenting a caricature nor a distorted picture of the Jews here. He is describing Judaism in its own terms. In fact, in vv 25-29 Paul will give a description of the true Jew as one who keeps the law, and in chap. 3 he will talk about the advantage the Jew has over the non-Jew (see 3:1-3). Being a Jew, following the law, and boasting in one's relation with God are presented here in a descriptive, neutral, or even somewhat positive manner.

This means that in Romans 2:17-20 Paul is not critcizing the Jew for boasting. Paul's attitude toward boasting will have undergone some severe transformation by the time we reach 3:27, in which boasting is excluded. But for the moment, at Romans 2:17, boasting in a right relation to God based on obedience to the law is not under attack.

It is interesting to note that the connection between boasting and law which we see in 2:17 is also reproduced at 3:27, where boasting will be excluded by some kind of law (the RSV says that boasting is excluded by the "principle of faith," but the Greek text more literally says "law [*nomos*] of faith;" we shall discuss this term below). Thus, the link between Romans 3:27 and 2:17 is derived not only from the presence of the same terms but also by the relationship between those terms: boasting and its dependence on the law. It is precisely this link that indicates what Paul means by boasting. For Paul, boasting exhibits a confidence in the rightness of one's relationship with God, a sense of security, or even privilege, that is based on one's faithful adherence to the demands of the law of Moses. This boasting is a specifically Jewish trait, because it is a characteristic of Jews who obey the law of Moses. "Boasting" in Romans 2:17 and 3:27 is not a general human characteristic based on self-aggrandizement, nor does it refer to an exaggerated attempt by the Jews to obey the law without the help of the grace of God, as it has sometimes been misunderstood in the past. Boasting, to be sure, is related to following the law, but as Romans 2:17 clearly suggests, Paul has no quarrel with that concept, in and of itself.

We see, then, that we must modify our first understanding of boasting as referring to sinful human pride. For Paul, the meaning is much narrower: boasting is a Jewish confidence in one's relationship with God based on faithful obedience to the Mosaic law.

If Paul has no quarrels with the idea of the Jew boasting in God and relying on the law in Romans 2:17, why then does he announce the absolute exclusion of that same boasting in Romans 3:27? We shall see that Paul actually provides a double reason why boasting is excluded. We can summarize his double argument briefly before presenting it in greater detail. First, Paul, excoriates the Jews for their boasts in the law because, in actual fact, they do not obey the law. However acceptable the theory of a confidence in God that is based on one's obedience to the law may be, the fact of the matter is that such confidence is absurd if one is actually disobeying the law. And for Paul, this is clearly the case. Paul's second reason for the exclusion of boasting in Romans 3:27 will focus on the revelation of God in Jesus Christ. This gracious intervention has completely shifted the whole question of confidence in one's relationship to God away from following the law and has thus provided a new basis for all relationships to God: faith in Jesus Christ. Obedience to the law (or even lack of obedience to the law) is no longer the fundamental question in terms of right relations with God. The only basis for that relationship is faith in Christ.

We have summarized in broad outline Paul's argument from his mention of boasting at Romans 2:17 to his radical conclusion about its exclusion in 3:27. We will now present a more detailed exposition of this discussion.

C. Paul's First Criticism of Boasting: Romans 2:17-3:20

Although we have indicated that at Romans 2:17 Paul seems to have no quarrel with boasting in and of itself, at the same time we are making a qualification when we talk about boasting "in and of itself." This qualification immediately suggests that there can be situations in which boasting is unacceptable. That Paul is primarily interested in the conditions under which boasting should be condemned appears in Romans 2:17, where Paul's neutral description of Jewish boasting occurs within a very important conditional ("if. . . , then. . . ") clause.[3]

---

[3]Although it is legitimate to understand Rom 2:17 as initiating an "if . . . then" construction, the "then" is only implied (at Rom 2:21). See Jouette M. Bassler, *Divine*

In the long protasis (the "if" part, vv 17-19), Paul uses a number of images favorable to his Jewish audience: relying on the law and boasting in God, knowing God's will and approving what is excellent, acting as a guide and teacher to others because of knowledge of the law and of the truth. Compliment is added to compliment in this litany of praise for the Jews. But Paul leads his readers to the top of the mountain only to dash them from its lofty heights with a ringing challenge in the apodosis (the "then" part of the condition, implied here): "You who teach others, will you not teach yourself?" (v 21). Do you condemn stealing, he continues, and then steal? Do you condemn adultery, and then commit adultery? Do you condemn idolatry, and then collect idols? Do you boast in the law, and then dishonor God by breaking the law (vv 22-23)? Paul's clear implication is that any such behavior would be absurd.

Surely everyone agrees, Paul continues, that the real Jew is the one who obeys, rather than disobeys, the law. This truth is of such fundamental importance that even the person who does not bear the physical mark of Jewish identity (circumcision) but who nevertheless obeys the law of Moses can be considered a real Jew (vv 25-29). For Paul, faithful obedience to the law of Moses is the primary condition for true Jewish identity and thus the necessary basis on which any boasting might occur.

But Paul also knows that, in reality, it is precisely this faithful obedience to the law of Moses that is glaringly lacking from Jewish life, and thus the basis for boasting is reduced to an illusion. Boasting in God while obeying the law may be acceptable, but boasting in God while transgressing the law is, quite simply, a lie.

This negative assessment which Paul makes on his Jewish contemporaries will culminate in Romans 3:19-20, after an extended series of quotations from the OT. After depicting the universality of sin within the Jewish world (3:10-18), Paul concludes in vv 19-20 that, however true it may be that the law of Moses offers a person the *opportunity* for faithful obedience,

Impartiality. Paul and a Theological Axiom, SBL Dissertation Series 59, Chico: Scholars Press, 1982, p. 262, n. 99.

the harsh reality is something far from obedience. The law "stops every mouth" (from boasting) and places everyone under the judgment of God, because through the law comes, not obedience, but the knowledge of sin (3:19-20).

This doleful conclusion which is explicitly expressed in 3:19-20 had already been anticipated earlier in the discussion of boasting. Shortly after Paul first mentioned boasting in 2:17, he asks pointedly, "You who boast in the law, do you dishonor God by breaking the law?" (2:23). Whatever truth there may be in boasting based in obedience to law, the reality is quite otherwise: obedience may fit the theory, but transgression pervades the reality.

We must be very clear in understanding what Paul is saying. On the one hand, we must note that Paul does not condemn boasting based on obedience. Nowhere does Paul say, Yes, you obey the law faithfully, and still your boasts are invalid. On the other hand, we must acknowledge Paul's unequivocal condemnation of boasting in the face of transgression. And yet, at Rom 3:27, Paul denies that boasting is excluded because of the law. Where, then, is the real source of his condemnation to be found?

Before answering that question, let us set out the broad lines of our argument thus far. In Rom 2:17-3:20 Paul has shown that the Jews may not boast in God based on their obedience to the law because in fact they transgress that law. The question of 3:27 could be posed immediately after 3:20 (temporarily eliminating 3:21-26 from the discussion), and in that case 3:27 would run something like this (we paraphrase): "Then what becomes of our boasting? It is excluded. On what principle? On the principle of works? Yes, the law excludes boasting since you do not obey the law and you thus have no works on which to base your boast."

This partial rewriting of Romans 3:27 is completely consistent with Paul's argumentation in Romans 2:17-3:20: you say you boast because you obey the law; but in fact you don't obey the law; therefore, the law itself is the basis which renders your boast invalid.

There is, however, one obvious problem with this proposed reconstruction of Romans 3:27; it represents in fact the complete opposite of what Paul actually says. For, as we have already noted, when Paul asks specifically if boasting is excluded by the law of works, he answers with an emphatic "No." He maintains, no doubt to his readers' surprise, that boasting is not excluded by the law.

Where, then, have we gone wrong in our reading of Paul's previous argumentation in 2:17-3:20? Has Paul argued there that boasting has no place if you don't obey the law, only to contradict himself in 3:27? Before we can resolve this apparent contradiction between our understanding of 2:17-3:20 and Paul's explicit and clear statement in 3:27, we must turn to a second argument which Paul constructs against Jewish boasting, a completely new argument that disregards the whole question of the law, which is found in 3:21-26.

D. Paul's Second Criticism of Jewish Boasting: Romans 3:21-26

Paul dramatically announces a new era in the history of humanity's relationship with God in Romans 3:21: "But now the righteousness of God has been manifested apart from law." Three points must be made here. First, the revelation of God's righteousness is a new action within history that is now revealed, as Paul will show, in the cross of Jesus (3:24-25). Second, this action is needed because the world's situation is hopeless: no human being is without sin. Help can only come from a new divine initiative. Third, the basis of this justifying action on God's part is most definitely not the law of Moses (see "apart from law" in 3:21). This means that the whole question of the law—whether it is obeyed or not—no longer forms the fundamental ground from which to judge one's relationship with God. As 3:24-26 will show, the basis for a right relationship with God is now rooted, not in law, but in faith in Jesus Christ.

The irrelevance of the Jewish law for the new basis for relating to God in v 21 can also be seen in certain details of Paul's argument in 3:21-26. First, Pauls affirms that the justifying righteousness of God is intended for "all who believe" (v 22).

The gracious action of God is directed to the whole world, not simply to the Jews, who possessed the law of Moses.

Second, this universal element of God's activity is further underscored by Paul's statement that not only is justification for all who believe, but also that "there is no distinction (*diastolē*) since all have sinned" (vv 22-23). What "distinction" is Paul referring to? The only other text in Romans in which Paul uses the word occurs at 10:12: "For there is no distinction between Jew and Greek." That this same sense is intended at 3:22 can be seen in Paul's reference to both Jews and Greeks under the power of sin at 3:9. Just as sin encompasses the whole world without distinction (3:9), so too God's justification is offered to the whole world without distinction (3:22). Thus, the offer of justification cannot depend on the Mosaic law, which would limit it to the Jewish world. Rather, it is directed to everyone.

Third, Paul announces that all persons are now justified, not on the basis of the law, but "freely" (*dōrean*; v 24). The conclusion must be drawn that even those who possess the law and even those who would obey it, now share in God's justification freely, neither because of the law, nor because of a supposed obedience to the law.

And fourth, Paul makes the new basis for the relation with God explicit. It is faith in Jesus Christ by which one is made righteous. Faith, not law, is the ground of justification (see vv 22 and 26).

In short, Romans 3:21-26 presents a criticism of Jewish boasting in God based on following the law by demonstrating that the law is simply irrelevant to the question of one's relationship with God. In addition, Paul completely prescinds from the question as to whether that law is obeyed or not. In either case, the law forms no part in the process of the revelation of God's justifying righteousness.

This, then, is Paul's second criticism of Jewish boasting, a completely Christocentric attack that makes the question of the law irrelevant. The exclusive focus on faith in Jesus Christ in 3:21-26 renders his first attack (2:17-3:20: boasting is excluded because of disobedience) quite pointless. If it is true that faith in Christ is the basis of everyone's relation with God, then, possession of the Mosaic law, obedience to it, or even transgression of it, are no longer elements by which to determine whether or not one can "boast" in one's relation to God. Thus, in a more profound manner than had ever been hinted at in 2:17-3:20 (in which the realities of sinful history provided the alleged basis for the exclusion of boasting), we now realize that boasting is excluded, not in fact by the law of works (however accurate this explanation may be in itself), but rather, boasting is excluded by faith. The whole question of the law is beside the point. And this is precisely what Paul says in Romans 3:27.

We have seen that Paul criticizes Jewish boasting from two perspectives. The first might be called the "Jewish" perspective: even Jews must admit the futility of boasting in the face of such widespread and apparent disobedience (2:17-3:20). The second perspective from which Paul criticizes boasting is uniquely Christian. Boasting is eliminated because law and works are no longer relevant to the fundamental ground of one's relationship with God; all that matters is faith in Jesus Christ (3:21-26). In Romans 3:27 Paul recapitulates his first attack on boasting by asking if boasting is excluded by the "law of works" or the Mosaic law. If we forget about the argument of 3:21-26, we can legitimately expect a positive answer to this question: Yes, the Mosaic law excludes boasting because the Mosaic law is not obeyed. But drawing 3:21-26 back into the discussion, as we surely must, we are forced to reconsider Paul's question about boasting and the law. Now, in light of God's revelation in Christ, we must say that indeed, boasting is not excluded by the law of works, but is rather excluded by faith. Paul has shifted the focal points of the discussion of justification from human activity (or lack of it: 2:17-3:20) to divine activity (3:21-26).

Thus, what at first appeared to be a contradiction between 2:17-3:20 (boasting is excluded by law) and 3:27 (boasting is not excluded by law) is now seen to be understandable in terms of the intervening verses, 3:21-26. Paul very deftly moved from a Jewish critique of boasting (2:17-3:20) to a Christian critique of boasting (3:21-26). This shift is quite clearly indicated in the vocabulary of Romans 3:27 itself, specifically in Paul's use of a standard "no, but rather" (*ouchi, alla*) pattern. By means of this expression, Paul is able to contradict an opinion that might be expected (boasting is indeed excluded by the lack of obedience to the law) and to propose a surprising and unexpected answer (boasting is excluded, not by law, but by faith). To see this shift clearly, we must investigate the language of v 27 more closely now.

E. The Shift Within Romans 3:27

In discerning a shift from Paul's first critique of boasting to his second critique within 3:27 itself, we must return to the introductory "then"(*oun*) in that verse. With our realization that in fact Paul has argued against boasting from a dual perspective and knowing that his second perspective really vitiates his first, we can now paraphrase Romans 3:27 as asking, "Now, in light of what has just been said in the second critique (3:21-26), is the first critique (2:17-3:20) still valid? Is boasting *still* excluded by the law (as first argued)? No, now, in the light of the revelation in Christ, boasting is excluded by faith."

It appears that Paul has carefully argued for the exclusion of boasting based on transgression of the law in 2:17-3:20 only to abandon that argument finally in 3:27. That this was indeed his intention is indicated by his use of the expression "no, but rather" (*ouchi, alla*). By means of this construction Paul wanted to show that however reasonable it may appear to say that boasting is excluded by law, however well-founded this answer may *seem* in view of his own argumentation, in fact, a new, more fundamental, and perhaps unexpected answer must be given to the question, How is boasting excluded?

In order to appreciate the significance of the "no, but rather" language in Romans 3:27, we must first contrast it with an expression that is more common in Paul, a simple "not this, but that") (*ou. . .alla. . .*) construction. At Romans 2:13: for example, Paul states that it is "*not the hearers* of the law who are righteous before God *but the doers* of the law who will be justified." Elsewhere, Paul writes that a worker's wages are "*not reckoned as a gift but as his due.*" (Rom 4:4). Later, Paul claims that Abraham's faith was reckoned as righteousness "*not after but before"* he was circumcised (Rom 4:10; see also 4:13, 20). In each of these examples one reality or idea is denied and another put in its place: not the hearers, but the doers; not as gift, but as his due; and so on. The contrast is simply "not this, but that." Paul also once uses the "*ouchi, alla*" pattern (the same pattern as in Rom 3:27) in the same way: " not your conscience but his" (1 Cor 10:29). But this simple negation/affirmation pattern is *not* the sense of the construction used in Romans 3:27. For there Paul uses the "no, but rather" pattern in an absolute way, and this absolute pattern has a quite different function in its uses in the NT.

What do we mean by an "absolute" use of *ouchi, alla*? By absolute use we refer to the situation in which a question is negated by "no, but rather." This is different from use of *ou...
alla...* in which one concept is negated and another concept put in its place. To understand Romans 3:27, we must investigate the absolute use of *ouchi, alla* elsewhere in the NT.

The absolute use of *ouchi, alla* occurs only once in Paul, at Romans 3:27. But it occurs six times in the gospels, and in each case it is used in the same way. Since the use of *ouchi, alla* is so consistent in these texts, we feel justified in applying what must be a standard meaning of the phrase to its use in Romans 3:27. We now look at each of these instances from the gospels.

Our first text is from the gospel of Luke. After the birth of John the Baptist everyone expects that, in accord with the custom of the time, the child would be named after his father, i.e., Zachary. This expectation is overturned, however, by the child's mother. She responds to those present by using the emphatic *ouchi, alla* pattern: "*Not so*; *but* he shall be called John" (Lk 1:60). Later in the gospel, when Jesus asks, "Do you think that I have come to give peace on earth," the expectation that he had indeed come for this purpose is denied, once again, with *ouchi, alla*; "*No*, I tell you, *but rather* division" (Lk 12:51). In our third example, the common assumption of the first-century world that evil befalls sinners is also challenged by means of the *ouchi, alla* pattern: concerning the Galileans who were slaughtered by Pilate and the unfortunate people upon whom the tower of Siloam fell, Jesus asks his disciples if they think that these people were necessarily worse sinners than anyone else. He then answers the question himself: "*No*, I tell you, *but* unless you repent you will all likewise perish" (Lk 13:3,5). In the story of the rich man and Lazarus, Father Abraham suggests to the rich man that Moses and the prophets are sufficient to encourage the man's family to repentance. But the rich man insists, "*No*, Father Abraham, *but* if someone goes to them from the dead, they will repent" (Lk 16:30). Finally, after the cure of the man born blind in John 9, there is some confusion in the crowd as to whether or not the healed man is really the same person as the man who had been blind: "Is not this the man who used to sit and beg?" Some said, "It is he;" others said, "*No, but* he is like him."

What is the comon thread which binds all of these examples of the absolute use of *ouchi, alla* together?[4] In each case, a situation occurs in which an expectation, and even a reasonable expectation, is reversed; the answer that may *seem* to be the most reasonable answer is in fact the wrong answer. Moreover, in many cases the expectation represents what we might call the "common sense" position or the "majority" view—that children are named after their parents, that Jesus came for peace rather than division, that misfortune befalls sinners as punishment, that Moses and the prophets effectively encourage repentance, etc. But in each case, the prevailing opinion is wrong, and the reader or hearer is shifted away from this incorrect view to a new, sometimes quite surprising view.

In Romans 3:27, the same kind of shift is evident. First, a question about boasting is posed. Then the exclusion of boasting is announced. How has this exclusion been accomplished? By a law of works? Just when the reader might expect a positive answer to this question based on Paul's own reasoning in 2:17-3:20, an abrupt shift appears in the line of thought, indicated once again by the *ouchi, alla* pattern: *No, but rather* by a law of faith. Once again, *ouchi, alla* signals a reversal of an expectation,

---

[4]Occasionally the *ouchi* and the *alla* are separated by direct address (e.g. Lk 16:30) or by some other parenthetical remark (e.g. "I tell you" in Lk 12:51). This does not invalidate our approach to the words as a unit.

and this time, an expectation based on Paul's own thought.

This shift in the reasoning in Romans 3:27 which is founded on Paul's argument starting back at 2:17, is also indicated by the term which the RSV translates as "principle," the Greek word *nomos*. Normally, the Greek *nomos* is translated by the English word "law." Thus a literal rendering of Romans 3:27 would be: "Where then is boasting? It has been excluded. Through what kind of law? [A law] of works? No, but rather through a law of faith." When we retain "law" as the translation for *nomos* then we can easily see that the connection between boasting and law initiated at Romans 2:17-23 has been carried into the conclusion of the discussion at Romans 3:27.

But the RSV is correct in translating *nomos* with "principle"; the word may also bear this meaning. Actually, a combination of our literal translation of the verse and the RSV translation might best illustrate the shift in Paul's thinking. Thus, when Paul asks, "Through what kind of *nomos* is boasting eliminated," he is surely thinking of the Mosaic *nomos* or law (as the further question, "Of works?" indicates). By using the term *nomos* in its most common meaning as the law of Moses Paul can remind his readers of his first critique of boasting and its exclusion through disobedience to that law. But at the same time, by using the word *nomos*, Paul can also point his readers *away* from this first critique (which is based on the *law* of works). Paul himself will neglect it because of his second critique (which is based on the *principle* of faith). In Greek, the words for "law" and "principle" here are the same (*nomos*), and Paul is using the word's double meaning to describe his double critique of Jewish boasting. The first is related to obedience to *law*; the second is related to the *principle* of faith. In the RSV translation, unfortunately, Paul's play on these words is no longer apparent.

We can also see that Paul immediately qualifies the meaning of *nomos* in Romans 3:27 the first time he uses it by asking, "Through *what kind of nomos*" is boasting excluded? In other words, Paul acknowledges that there is more than one kind of *nomos*. Is he perhaps preparing his readers here for his own double use of the term, meaning first "law" and then "principle"?

When Paul asks, "Through what kind of *nomos*", one's first reaction is to think of *nomos* as the Mosaic law, and this is partly correct. But one must also remember that *nomos* may be used in a more general sense, meaning "principle." This double sense of *nomos* ("law" as well as "principle") serves Paul's purpose very well. For he can use one and the same word to indicate his first critique of boasting based on "law" (*nomos*) as well as his second critique based on the "principle" (*nomos*) of faith. In 3:27 he refers to his first critique by asking "through what kind of *law*" and he then shifts to his second critique by answering "through the *principle* of faith." The shift from the first critique to the second is indicated not only by the explicit *ouchi, alla* terminology but also by the implicit shift in the meaning of *nomos* (from "law" to "principle") within the verse.[5]

CONCLUSION

We are now in a position to give an expanded rendering of Romans 3:27 that takes the full previous context of the verse quite seriously and at the same time captures the implications of its specific vocabulary: "Now then, in light of the new revelation of God in Christ which we just presented in 3:21-26, where is the boasting we first mentioned at 2:17? It is excluded. Through lack of obedience to the law of Moses (as we had originally argued in 2:17-3:20)? No! Now, because of the new revelation in Christ, boasting is excluded by faith." The question of the law, and obedience or lack of obedience to it, no longer enters the picture.

Paul has emphatically rejected a reasonable (but now irrelevant) answer to the question about boasting in favor of a gracious (and fundamental) answer. But this does not end the

---

[5]Some exegetes defend the position that *nomos* in Rom 3:27 refers both times to the law of Moses (see, e.g. C. Thomas Rhyne, *Faith Establishes the Law*, SBL Dissertation Series 55, Chico: Scholars Press, 1981, pp. 68-70). In our view, however, the "law of faith" can hardly refer to the law of Moses, particularly after 3:21, "apart from law." For a thorough study of the question, see, e.g., Heikki Räisänen, "Das Gesetz des Glaubens' (Röm 3, 27) und das 'Gesetz des Geistes' (Röm 8, 2) *New Testament Studies* 26 (1980) 101-17.

discussion. Paul continues, in the following verses, to strengthen his conclusion about boasting by drawing on both Jewish and Christian tradition. To these traditions we now turn.

Additional Note: An Alternative Understanding of "No"

When we discussed the question of 3:27 (Is boasting excluded through the Torah that requires works?), we indicated that the reader would expect the answer, "Yes, indeed; boasting is excluded through a law of works since the required works are not present; there is consequently absolutely no reason for boasting; boasting is excluded." Instead, Paul answers, "No, boasting is not excluded through the law of works!" In our explanation the "No" in v 27 is understood as "no *longer* by that Mosaic law of works, but rather by faith in Jesus Christ."

One may ask whether this "No" cannot be differently interpreted as follows: "Boasting would *not* be excluded if there were works." According to this way of reasoning, Paul theoretically agrees that obeying the law does not exclude acceptable boasting. Disobedience and, of course, redemption from sin freely given do exclude boasting.

A closer consideration of Rom 4:2 may support this understanding. In this verse, too, "works" and "boasting" are mentioned: "For if Abraham had been justified by works, he has something to boast about, but not before God." V 1 of the same chapter starts with a question: "What then shall we say that Abraham our forefather according to the flesh has found?" An answer is not immediately given but it can be supplied from the context. Abraham gained righteousness; more specifically, he found righteousness by way of gift, i.e., through faith.

The way Paul speaks in 4:2 may reveal how he understands the answer to the question of 3:27. Why is boasting excluded? Not through the law of works, not through the Torah which requires the keeping of the commandments. In Paul's mind the one who does the works of the law can call himself a true Jew: he can rely upon the Torah and boast of God and before God (cf. 2:17). So in principle, the law of works does not exclude boasting, although in reality boasting is ruled out in the first place because nobody has practiced nor practices all that the law asks.

In 2:17-3:20 the factual Jewish situation is depicted. At the end of 3:27, however, and in what follows, Paul no longer deals with the sins and shortcomings of the Jews. He points to God's new initiative which he indicates by means of the mysterious expression "the law of faith." Boasting is manifestly, primarily, and completely excluded by the law of faith, i.e., through a new "law" or dispensation in which faith is the central principle.[6]

---

[6]On this Additional Note, see the study of Jan Lambrecht mentioned in n. 1. For a more thorough analysis of Rom 4 we refer to our Chapter Five. Although this alternative understanding of "No" in 3:27 certainly changes the line of thought within this verse, the general approach to 3:27-31 and its context, however, is not affected by it.

2

Paul's Use of Christian
And Jewish Tradition
Romans 3:28-30

[28]For we hold that a person is justified by faith apart from works of law. [29]Or is God the God of Jews only? Is he not the God of Gentiles also? Yes, of Gentiles also, [30]if indeed the God, who will justify the circumcised on the ground of their faith and the uncircumcised through their faith, is one.[1]

Paul's argument for the exclusion of boasting, which started at Romans 2:17, has reached its final culmination in Romans 3:27: boasting is excluded by faith. Paul then continues by grounding this exclusion of boasting in two elements of traditional teaching, one of which comes from Christian catechesis, the other of which has its origin in Jewish thought. This first traditional element appears in v 28 and expresses the Christian concept of justification by faith. The second piece of tradition appears in v 29 and asserts a traditional Jewish view of the sovereignty of God. In v 30 Paul will draw on a further element in Jewish tradition, the idea of the oneness of God, and show how this belief joins with Christian tradition to support Paul's

---

[1]Our translation differs from that found in the RSV; for an explanation of this translation, see pp. 37-39.

main argument about the exclusion of boasting and its implications.

It might be well to point out here that it is the *implication* of the exclusion of Jewish boasting in a sense of privilege that is the most important idea in Romans 3:27-31. From our discussion of v 27 in the previous chapter, one might have the impression that boasting itself is Paul's main concern in this pericope. But we shall see in our discussion of vv 28-30 that Paul is actually leading his readers to a much broader and more fundamental point, namely that the elimination of any false sense of Jewish privilege or superiority necessarily leads to the conclusion that all men and women, Jews and non-Jews alike, are included in God's justifying action in Jesus Christ. This understanding of justification as a universal event, not limited to members of the Mosaic covenant (i.e. the Jews), is Paul's primary point in Romans 3:27-31, and follows directly from his initial assessment of boasting summed up in 3:27.

In our analysis of vv 28-30 we shall see how Paul moves from his negative evaluation of Jewish boasting to his positive assessment of the universality of justification offered in Jesus.

A. Pauls Draws on Christian Tradition (v 28)

In v 28 Paul draws on the common Christian belief that justification is by faith in support of his previous judgment about the exclusion of boasting. The function of v 28 as a supporting statement for v 27 is apparent in the first word of the verse, the conjunction "for" (*gar*). This word indicates that the content of this verse is to be understood as support for what has preceded.[2] While the exclusion of boasting (v 27) might be

---

[2]At first sight, the Greek text of Rom 3:28 is not as clear as our English rendering of it. Some mss. read "therefore" (*oun*) in place of "for" (*gar* as if 3:28 were a conclusion *derived* from 3:27 rather than a statement *supporting* it. The external evidence of the Greek manuscripts themselves slightly favors "for," and commentators are in agreement that this is indeed the original wording of the sentence (see Bruce M. Metzger, *A Textual Commentary on the Greek New Testament*, London/New York: United Bible Society, 1971, p. 509).

somewhat novel to Paul's Jewish-Christian readers at Rome, the basis on which he makes the teaching is not. If Paul is trying to support his point in v 27 with v 28, it makes sense for us to think that v 28 is not itself a matter of dispute. We must assume, therefore, that Paul's readers will not dispute that justification is by faith.

Furthermore, we can clearly see that Paul assumes that everyone will agree with what he says in v 28 from the specific vocabulary he uses in that verse. When Paul uses the phrase "we hold" (*logizometha*) he is indicating that what is here presented is something with which all his readers could be expected to agree, that what he is saying is already fixed teaching in the church. Commentators generally agree on this meaning for Paul's wording here, but the significance of it has often gone unrecognized.[3] We can safely assume that Paul expects his audience to agree that God justifies on the basis of faith. Paul draws on this common belief as support for his contention that boasting is eliminated.

If we are right in understanding v 28 as a general statement with which everyone already agreed, then a very important conclusion follows. Paul is *not* introducing his teaching on justification by faith here as the main point of his argument. Rather, he is using this already accepted teaching on justification by faith (which he has outlined in 3:21-26) in support of something else, namely, the exclusion of boasting.

The main point of Paul's argument in 3:27-31, then, is not justification by faith (as important as this concept may be in Pauline thought in general). The specific teaching of 3:27-31 is the exclusion of boasting, and Paul uses his doctrine of justification by faith to support that teaching. In arguing against Jewish privilege based on possession of the Mosaic law Paul draws on what everyone knows, namely that God justifies on the basis of faith, and therefore any sense of privileged status connected with the law is out of place. In v 28 Paul agrees that if

[3]See Richard B. Hays, 'Have We Found Abraham to Be Our Forefather According to the Flesh?' A Reconstruction of Rom 4:1," *Novum Testamentum* 27 (1985) 76-98, p. 85.

justification is by faith, then boasting in one's privileged status based on law makes no sense.

But in v 28 Paul also provides us with a fundamental basis on which to conclude that boasting is excluded in another way as well. The point is not only *that* God justifies by faith, but *whom* he justifies by faith. Paul does not specify that God justifies *only Jews* in this way, but that he justifies *everyone* in this way. For we hold that *a person* (= every person; RSV: "a man"; *anthrôpon*) is justified by faith apart from works of law." The statement is quite general, and certainly not limited only to the Jews. Without making it explicit at this point, Paul is nonetheless steadily moving toward his corollary to the exclusion of boasting, namely, the inclusion of all people in God's gracious action in Jesus Christ.

Before we take up the more explicit treatment of the inclusion of all people in justification (which will be spelled out in vv 29-30) it might be helpful to summarize Paul's argument about the exclusion of boasting up to this point. In Rom 2:17-3:20 Paul argued that boasting is excluded because of disobedience to the law. In 3:21-26, Paul showed that this lack of obedience is no longer his focus, since the basis of all relationships with God is now faith rather than obedience. Paul affirms this double critique in 3:27, and summarizes it once again in 3:28. To paraphrase that verse, "We believe that one is justified by faith (as stated in 3:21-26) rather than by works of law (which was treated in 2:17-3:20)."

Paul's understanding of boasting should be manifestly clear at this point and he can therefore take this moment to move to a new stage in his argument. This he does in v 29.

B. Paul Draws on Jewish Tradition (v 29)

Paul no doubt assumes that his readers will be following his argument as he presents it, and will see the cogency of his reasoning. In v 29, however, he presents the alternative conclusion which must be drawn by anyone who might disagree with his attack on boasting. He highlights this false conclusion by beginning this sentence with the disjunctive particle "or" *(ē)*. This word tells the reader that if he or she is not in agreement with Paul so far, then the following conclusion must be drawn: God is only the God of the Jews and not the God of the Gentiles. For Paul, if you deny that justification for everyone is by faith (v 28) and if you deny that boasting in a privileged position before God has been eliminated (v 27), then you cannot avoid the conclusion that God is really only the God of the Jews. It would be impossible to maintain that Jewish status still gives one a privileged relation to God and at the same time to maintain that God is equally the God of all peoples.

Paul was fairly confident that no one would fall prey to this false conclusion, believing that God was not the God of everyone. His enthusiastic language in the rest of the verse confirms this, for he continues (we paraphrase), "God is the God of the Gentiles as well, isn't he? Of course he is!"

Now it would be grossly unfair to think that the typical Jew would ever deny God's universal sovereignty over all humanity, at least as regards creating and judging the world. In terms of creation and judgment, God was surely the God of everyone and Paul uses this traditional Jewish understanding of God as part of his argument. And yet, the Jews were unwilling to forfeit their sense of some special relationship with God based on their possession of his own law. Rabbi Simeon ben Jochai, who lived during the middle of the second century, summed up this typical Jewish feeling about God: "I am God over all that come into the world but I have joined by name only with you; I am not called the God of the idolaters, but the God of Israel" (*ExodusRabbah* 29:88d). Surely God must love the Jews in some special way; had he not demonstrated that by giving them his law?

Paul has questioned this line of thinking from two perspectives. First, the Jews don't obey the law anyway; and second, the new basis for every relationship with God is now faith in Christ, not law. In vv 29-30, in which Paul draws on both Christian and Jewish traditional ideas, he very subtly introduces into the discussion the most radical conclusion he wishes to draw. Not only is boasting excluded and Jewish privilege thereby undermined, but more positively, God is shown to be the God of the

Gentiles as well as the God of the Jews.

It is this very idea—that God is equally the God of Jew and non-Jew alike—that contains Paul's crucial insight into what God has achieved in Jesus Christ. Ever since the events on Calvary, ever since the manifestation of God's righteousness in the cross of Jesus, no one can claim any decisive closeness to God simply because he or she is a Jew. To maintain such a sense of "specialness," to go so far as to "boast" in the privilege, is deeply wrong because the Jew is also a sinner. Such reasoning leads to two untenable conclusions. First, God really does not justify all persons on the basis of faith; and second, God is somehow more the God of Jews than the God of non-Jews. Since we know that both of these conclusions are false, Paul argues, the basis for any sense of privilege must have been eliminated.

This universalistic understanding of God's relationship with humanity, this broadening of God's act of justification to Jew and non-Jew alike on an equal basis, is the positive corollary that necessarily follows from Paul's arguments against boasting. But Paul has not finished presenting his case just yet; he will draw on one more element of traditional Jewish thought, one might say the most fundamental element of that thought, and interpret it in light of the Christian teaching on justification by faith.

C. Paul Combines Christian and Jewish Tradition (v 30)

While steadily drawing his readers toward his conclusions about the universality of God's love, Paul now moves to the fundamental theological notion on which Judaism rests, the oneness of God. The importance of the belief that God is one can be seen in the ordinary life of the Jew, who every morning began the day with Israel's greatest prayer, known as the Shema; "Hear O Israel, the Lord our God is one Lord." The text of the prayer can be found in Deuteronomy 6:4, and the first word of the prayer in Hebrew gives it its name: *shema* (hear).

This affirmation of the one God was not only part of the

prescribed daily prayer of the faithful Jew (see Mishna tractate *Berakoth*), but this prayer also formed part of the texts of Scripture that were enclosed in the phylacteries, the small boxes which the Jews wore on their forehead and left arm during prayer. These same texts were also placed in the *mezuzah*, the tiny case affixed to the doorpost of a Jewish house. Jesus himself quoted the Shema when he was asked which was the greatest commandment (Mk 12:29). The centrality of the idea of the oneness of God permeated every aspect of Jewish life.

Paul now rests his case for the unversality of justification (and thus the elimination of Jewish boasting) on this most fundamental tenet of Judaism itself. But in order to penetrate the line of thought in Paul's argument in v 30 we must first see how the translation of this verse in the RSV obscures what Paul is really trying to say. Before we provide a more literal translation of the verse let us look at the reasoning as it appears in the RSV text.

In the RSV, v 30 appears to be a continuation of v 29, providing a reason why God can be considered the God of the Gentiles: "since God is one." The RSV then adds a second thought to this affirmation of the oneness of God: "and he will justify the circumcised on the ground of their faith and the uncircumcised through their faith." In this translation, Paul seems to be saying two things: first, that God is one; and second, that God will justify on the basis of faith. The problem in interpreting the text enters the picture when we ask how these two ideas are related to one another.

Exegetes commonly read Romans 3:30 "causally," i.e., they interpret the verse to mean that *because* God is one, therefore he will justify all humanity on one and the same basis.[4] Some scholars, however, point the line of reasoning in the opposite direction, but preserve the causal sense. They maintain that since God will justify on the one basis of faith, therefore he is truly revealed as the one God.[5] Which of these two interpretations is correct?

---

[4] See, for example, Jouette M. Bassler, "Divine Impartiality in Paul's Letter to the Romans," *Novum Testamentum* 26 (1984) 43-58, especially p. 55.

[5] See, for example, the commentary of Ulrich Wilckens, *Der Brief an die Römer*,

Two points argue against the first one. We have already seen
that justification by faith is not the new conclusion which Paul
wishes to present to his readers in this section of Romans. On
the contrary, justification by faith is something that he assumes
every reader already believes (see v 29). Therefore, there is no
reason to think that the idea of justification by faith is being
introduced as something new in v 30. Furthermore, this first
interpretation does not do justice to the grammar of the Greek
text. How, then, should the verse be understood?

The correct understanding of this text can be seen when we
make a translation of v 30 that is more literal than the one in the
RSV: "if indeed the God who will justify the circumcised by
faith and the uncircumcised through faith is one." In this translation, v 30 still remains a supporting statement for v 29 (note
the beginning: "if indeed"; it refers, as it were, to an insight which
will be accepted by all readers). Further, and more importantly,
we no longer have two somewhat independent statements about
God, as in the RSV text ([1] God is one and [2] he will justify by
faith). Rather, in our translation Paul's statement in v 30 is
essentially *one* statement (God is one) with an accompanying
relative clause describing how this God will justify Jew and
non-Jew alike (because of faith).

The protasis in v 30 is simply this: if God is one. The relative
clause, "who will justify..." (grammatically, a clause dependent
on "God"), is a secondary description of God, and not, as the
RSV has it, a second independent affirmation about God. The
if-clause affirming the oneness of God and the relative clause
describing God are both used grammatically to support the final
affirmation of v 29, that God is the God of the Gentiles: "*if
indeed* this God who will justify ... by faith is one.*"

This means that v 30 actually makes one statement about the
God who justifies by faith. He is one. This statement is itself
used to support the affirmation of v 29: God is God of the
Gentiles. In effect, then, we are rejecting the idea that v 30
contains a relationship in which the first statement is a premise

Evangelisch-Katholischer Kommentar Zum Neuen Testament 6/1, Zurich: Benziger
Verlag and Neukirchen-Vluyn: Neukirchener Verlag 1978, p. 248.

and the second a conclusion drawn from it, as in the following scheme:

Premise	*Conclusion*
God is one	therefore he will justify everyone by faith.

V 30, contains the simple affirmation that God is one, and in the course of this affirmation the verse describes this one God as he who will justify everyone on the basis of faith. By means of this common affirmation that the God who will justify everyone by faith is one (v 30), Paul has drawn the innovative conclusion that he is really and equally the God of all men and women, Jews and Gentiles alike, as stated in v 29.[6]

The importance of this somewhat detailed grammatical analysis comes to the fore when one asks the simple question, What are vv 27-30 about? Many exegetes hold that this section of Romans is about justificaton by faith. We have seen, however, that justification by faith is *assumed* in these verses. It is not the point of contention. Paul's new teaching in Romans 3:27-30 is not that God justifies by faith (that was the content of 3:21-26), but rather that since the one God justifies everyone by faith, therefore he is the God of all, the Jew and non-Jew alike. It is the universality of justification, not its grounding in faith, that forms Paul's essential teaching in these verses.

In bringing his argument about universal justification to a conclusion in v 30, Paul has joined together the two most basic tenets of both Jewish and Christian faith, the Jewish conviction about the oneness of God and the Christian conviction about justification by faith. In melding these two traditions together, Paul has presented an unassailable case that God is, indeed, the God of all. As far as justification is concerned, no one, not even a Jew, has any special claim on God.

Our interpretation of v 30 emphasizes the main line of thought in it. Other smaller problems in this verse have also been discussed by scholars. Occasionally, for example, exegetes will

[6]The interpretation of v 30 which we defend here can also be found in the Dutch commentary of Herman Ridderbos, *Aan de Romeinen*, Kampen: Kok, 1959, p. 89.

question whether or not Paul really intended to say that both Jews and non-Jews are justified in *exactly* the same way, and they base this question on two different expressions in v 30. Note that Paul says the Jews ("the circumcised") will be justified *on the ground of* their faith, and non-Jews ("the uncircumcised") will be justified *through* their faith. One exegete has proposed that Paul is really saying here that the Jews are justified by faith, and the Gentiles are justified by that same faith, namely, by the faith of the Jews.[7] Another scholar proposes that the Jews are justified by sharing the faith of Abraham, while Gentiles are justified by sharing faith in the One who raised Jesus from the dead.[8] Is there any compelling reason to give so much significance to these different prepositional phrases, with the result that God really appears to justify Jews and non-Jews in different ways?

This question is probably to be answered negatively. Not only must the reader avoid the temptation to seek out special meaning for every detail of the biblical text, but he or she must also realize that sometimes writers vary their terminology only for stylistic reasons (to avoid repetition, for example). Most exegetes agree that the difference in the prepositions here is merely one of style. We can point to a text like Romans 3:20 as an example of similar variation. In that verse, the two phrases "by works of the law" and "through law" reproduce the same prepositions that we find in 3:30. But there is no difference in meaning between the two expressions. Similarly, in Romans 3:30 we may safely agree with the majority of commentators that the difference in prepositions here is purely rhetorical, i.e., without any difference in meaning.

A second question arises with regard to the future tense in v 30, "will justify." Is this future tense to be regarded as a real temporal future, pointing to some act of God that has not yet occurred but will only come at some later point in time? This is

---

[7]See Nigel Turner, *Grammatical Insights into the New Testament*, Edinburgh, 1965, pp. 107-10.

[8]Hendrikus Boers, "The Problem of Jews and Gentiles in the Macro-Structure of Romans," *Neotestamentica* 15 (1981) 1-11, pp. 7-8.

probably not the case. Since Paul affirms in 3:27 that boasting has already been excluded (note the past tense of the verb) it seems correct to understand the future tense in v 30 as a "logical future." Thus the verse means, "if (= since) the God who justifies by faith is one (he is God of all)." Paul is not actually postponing God's justifying activity, but is describing the actions of the one God who has already effected the exclusion of boasting in the cross of Jesus. The future tense here is not to be taken literally.

CONCLUSION

In our examination of Romans 3:28-30 we have seen Paul move from his initial statement about the exclusion of boasting in 3:27 to his radical conclusion about the universal and equal sovereignty of God over all human persons, irrespective of their status as Jews or non-Jews. In the course of his argument, Paul has marshalled evidence originating in the most fundamental aspects of the Jew's life, their identity as a people specially related to God, their possession of God's own law, and their unwavering faith in the oneness of that God.

Paul starts with the exclusive privileges of the Jews and proclaims that, in the light of the Christ event, justification no longer depends on these privileges. Is Paul then completely denying the validity of those privileges, thereby rejecting the idea that the Jews do possess the law? Is he, in effect destroying the validity of that very law? The weighty objections lie behind the accusation raised against Paul in v 31, and he answers them— negatively—in the strongest possible terms.

3

Paul's Teaching Upholds the Law
Romans 3:31

(a) Do we then overthrow the law by this faith?
(b) By no means!
(c) On the contrary, we uphold the law.

Thus far we have seen Paul's skillful interweaving of basic Christian and Jewish beliefs, the combination of which points to the conclusion that God is indeed the God of everyone. This central conviction, that in Christ there is "neither Jew nor Greek," formed the natural conclusion to the Pauline preaching of God's righteousness revealed in Jesus. But at Romans 3:31 the very soundness of Paul's argumentation seems to backfire on him. If Paul is right in his claim that there is no longer any basis for a sense of Jewish privilege with respect to God, then has he not in fact abolished the need for the entire Jewish religion, undermining the entire Mosaic covenant? More specifically, has Paul abolished the validity of the Mosaic law and thus rendered any sense of Jewish identity meaningless?

This is the objection levelled against him in the first part of v 31, and which he rhetorically poses as a question to himself: "Do we then overthrow the law by this faith?" In other words, Do we deny the importance of the law of Moses, and thereby make our whole Jewish past of no significance whatsoever?

Immediately after the question is raised, Paul vehemently rejects it by employing a standard formula of denial: God forbid!, in Greek *mê genoito* (literally: "may it not be so"). Paul uses this same formula at other places in his writings to reject what he thinks are absolutely untenable conclusions, often with regard to the same question being raised here. For example, Paul often raises questions about the validity of the law or the present significance of God's past dealings with Israel: Is the law itself sin? *mê genoito!* (Rom 7:7); Is God unjust for seeming to reject Israel? *mê genoito!* (Rom 9:14); Has God rejected his people? *mê genoito!* (Rom 11:1); Is the law against the promises of God? *mê genoito!* (Gal 3:21). Throughout his writings, Paul staunchly maintains that his teaching does not overthrow the meaning and validity of the Mosaic covenant.

But the very fact that Paul is so often forced to defend himself against essentially the same charge shows us that, at least to many of his hearers and readers, his teaching had the unsettling effect of appearing to deny what he so ardently tried to affirm. Contemporary readers of Paul's letters are no more convinced than were some of the original readers; exegetes still sense that Paul, in fact, "overthrows the law," no matter how hard he tries to deny the accusation.

Even when Paul specifically denies this very charge at Romans 3:31, and goes so far as to say that, on the contrary, he upholds the law (3:31c), some contemporary exegetes remain skeptical. Heikki Räisänen, for example, has recently affirmed that it is "scarcely possible" to understand Paul's positive statement about the law in Romans 3:31. Paul's claim to uphold the law is "both internally inconsistent and externally problematic." According to Räisänen, the retort in 3:31c does not really answer the charge in 3:31a; it "could only have deceived those who were already convinced."[1]

Räisänen's problems with Paul's text are substantial, and not without a solid foundation in Paul's own writings. We have

---

[1]Heikki Räisänen, *Paul and the Law*, Wissenschaftliche Untersuchungen zum Neuen Testament 29, Tübingen: J.C.B. Mohr, 1983, pp. 71-72.

already seen that Paul uses the most basic Jewish beliefs to argue against Jewish privilege and identity. How can Paul fail to see the inconsistency that seems so clear to others? Can Paul seriously think that he upholds the law?

Before we begin the process of answering this question more fully, we must state one methodological presupposition with regard to Romans 3:31: when Paul says that he upholds the law, we think that he meant it. He was not playing word games (shifting the meaning of "law," for example, from one meaning in the accusation of 3:31a to another meaning in 3:31c), nor was he merely tossing off the accusation of 3:31a without a serious consideration of it and an attempt to answer it. Whether or not he succeeded in that attempt is a judgment that each reader must make for himself or herself. But we take Paul seriously, however difficult it may be to follow his reasoning.

Our endeavor to understand this difficult verse will center on three questions, derived from recently scholarly research on Romans 3:31. First, how does the verse function in its context? Does it form the conclusion to the arguments of Romans 3, or is it better understood as the heading for Romans 4, directly leading to the discussion of Abraham there? Second, are "overthrow" and "uphold" technical terms, specifically, terms borrowed from rabbinic discussions about the law? Do they form a stereotyped pair? If so, what light do they shed on the way in which Paul understood his "upholding" the law? And finally, what precisely is the law which Paul is accused of overthrowing and which he maintains that he upholds? Does "law" here refer to the entire Jewish religion, the Mosaic covenant? Does it refer to the exemplary stories and legal prescriptions of the Pentateuch or perhaps the entire OT? Does it bear a more limited meaning, indicating only the legal prescriptions of the law, or perhaps only the moral demands of the law? Basically we must ask, when Paul claims that he upholds the law, what is it that he is upholding?

Our understanding of the meaning of the term "law" in Romans 3:31 actually plays a role in the other questions we have posed, and we will say a few words about it before discussing the function of Romans 3:31 in its context. The Greek word that Paul uses for "law," *nomos*, may bear a wide variety of meanings.

Occasionally it simply refers to a general "rule" or "principle," as in Rom 3:27 (see above p. 27). Elsewhere *nomos* indicates the OT Scripture, more specifically, the Pentateuch, encompassing both the stories of Israel's past as well as the specific legal prescriptions of the Mosaic law. A good example of this use can be seen in Romans 3:21: the revelation of God has been "witnessed by the law (*nomos*) and the prophets." Here *nomos* clearly refers to the Pentateuch. But *nomos* also appears in 3:21 with another meaning: the revelation of God has been manifested "apart from law (*nomos*)." In this phrase, the same Greek word that earlier referred to the entire Pentateuch ("witnessed by the law") now bears a more restricted meaning: the legal demands of the law of Moses (this meaning is drawn from the context of the previous discussion, in which *nomos* had this more limited meaning; see, e.g. 3:20). With this variety in the meaning of the Greek *nomos*, one can perceive the problems involved in understanding a deceptively simple statement like Romans 3:31. Which of these various possible understanding of *nomos* is the one Paul intended?

To simplify our discussion of Romans 3:31 the various understandings of *nomos* will be reduced to two: *nomos* as story (i.e., the stories in the Pentateuch) or *nomos* as stipulation (i.e., the laws in the Pentateuch, and of the Mosaic covenant generally).

Although we will devote a separate section of this chapter to discussing the meaning of *nomos*, we shall see that this question runs throughout the entire discussion of Romans 3:31. Thus it will already play a large part in our first section concerning the function of Romans 3:31 in its context. To that discussion we now turn.

A. The function of 3:31:
Conclusion to Romans 3 or Heading for Romans 4?

A large number of scholars believe that when Paul says he upholds the law he means that he affirms the continuing validity of Scripture for Christians and for the church. The Pentateuch is of special importance. It contains the stories of the great heroes of Jewish faith, the patriarchs Abraham, Isaac and Jacob. Most notable of the three is Abraham, whose importance Paul himself acknowledges when he calls Abraham the "father of us all"(Rom 4:16). Indeed, Paul specifically cites the example of Abraham in his discussions of faith and works in Romans 4, which immediately follows on Romans 3:31. Clearly then, some scholars argue, when Paul says that he upholds the law, he means that he upholds the Scripture by offering an interpretation of the story of Abraham, as found in Scripture, in Romans 4.²

This understanding of Romans 3:31 has been extensively argued by C. Thomas Rhyne in his published doctoral dissertation, *Faith Establishes the Law*.³ Since this position often appears in the exegesis of this verse, and since Rhyne provides a thorough defense of it, we will take him as representative of this understanding and examine his arguments in some detail.

We may begin by noting that in this interpretation of Romans 3:31 *nomos* is understood to be Scripture *as story*. Rhyne defends this understanding of *nomos* by pointing back to the phrase in Romans 3:21, which we have already mentioned, "the law (*nomos*) and the prophets." Here *nomos* is Scripture, specifically the Pentateuch. Rhyne further asserts that *nomos* in Romans 3:27 again refers to the Pentateuch, and the expression "law of faith" summarizes the function of the Scripture (i.e., the Pentateuch) as witnessing to the need for faith. Rhyne acknowledges that in 3:28, in the phrase "apart from works of law," *nomos* does not mean the stories of the Pentateuch, but he says this is merely part of the tension between faith and works which is present in Paul's thought.

Of course, Rhyne and others are correct in asserting that Paul believed that his own teaching generally affirmed the value of Scripture. Paul's constant reference to, and use of, the OT strikingly attests to his positive assessment of the Jewish Scriptures. But the question before us now is whether or not it is the validity of Scripture that is precisely at issue in Romans 3:31. Does *nomos* understood as Rhyne and many others present it

---

²This understanding of Rom 3:31 can be found, for example, in the commentaries of Frederick Fyvie Bruce and Ernst Käsemann.

³Society of Biblical Literature Dissertation Series, 55, Scholars Press: Chico, 1981.

make sense in this particular verse? We think that it does not.

We agree with Rhyne, however, when he focuses on the importance of the preceding context for understanding the meaning of *nomos* in Romans 3:31. But we disagree that the context demands an understanding of *nomos* as Scripture. On the contrary, it is precisely the prior context of Romans 3:31 that demands that *nomos* in that verse be understood in the more limited sense of a legal corpus, specifically, the legal demands of the law of Moses, rather than in the more general sense of the stories of the Pentateuch. Three lines of argumentation compel us to this conclusion.

First, although Rhyne's understanding of *nomos* may make sense in Romans 3:31*c* (We uphold the law as Scripture), in what possible way could the objection of 3:31*a* also refer to Paul's "overthrowing" the value of Scripture? Not only must the affirmation of v 31c become understandable in the context of the preceding material, but the objection of v 31a must equally flow from what Paul has been saying prior to that point. The previous context does not suggest an objection to Paul based on his refusal to grant the authority or validity of Scripture.

Second, the tension between faith and law in 3:31 is also present in 3:28: a person is justified by faith apart from works of law. In v 28 the "law" is clearly the legal demands of the Mosaic law, not Scripture. The same contrast is present in 3:27: boasting is excluded by faith rather than by the law which demands works, i.e., the Mosaic law. The logic of Paul's argument from 3:27-30 necessarily must lead up to the objection in 3:31a: if boasting is excluded by faith rather than by following the law (v 28), then do we therefore overthrow the Mosaic law by this faith (v 31)? The entire thrust of Paul's argument, beginning as it does already at Romans 2:17, concerns the Jews and their success or failure at following the demands of the Law (see especially 2:17-24). Paul argues that, in fact, this question about obedience to the law becomes irrelevant in the light of the cross of Jesus, but it is this very question that appears in v 31: if obedience to the law is no longer necessary for inclusion in the justifying action of God, then it apears that the law—as legal demand and not as story—is being rendered null and void.

Finally, Paul's positive attitude toward *nomos* as story or Scripture is so apparent throughout the letter to the Romans that one is hardly able to believe that he would be accused of overthrowing the Scripture in 3:31a. The implicit reference to Deuteronomy 6:4, the Shema, in v 30, tells against this understanding of v 31. Furthermore, the validity of Scripture has already been well established before 3:31, not only implicitly with the extended citation of the OT at 3:10-18, but explicitly at the very opening of the letter: the gospel was already promised through the prophets in the Holy Scriptures (1:2). This positive view of the OT is echoed at 3:21: the present revelation is witnessed by the law and the prophets. Paul's clear affirmation of the value of Scripture makes it unlikely that in Romans 3:31a a question is posed precisely about the value of Scripture.

Essentially, our criticism of Rhyne here is that, while Rhyne's interpretation of *nomos* as Scripture *could* make sense in 3:31*c*, it does not make sense in 3:31*a*. The preceding context raises a question about Paul's attitude toward the legal elements of the law; it does not call into doubt Paul's attitude toward Scripture. The question about overthrowing the "law" cannot reasonably refer to Scripture.

criticism of him. He writes that Paul is "concerned with preserving the validity of the law in *view of his blatant rejection of its presumed role in salvation*" (emphasis added). According to Rhyne's own interpretation, then, since the "law" refers to Scripture, Paul must blatantly reject the role of *Scripture* in salvation. But, as we have seen, Paul never questions the role of Scripture, but only the role of the legal demands of the law of Moses. Thus, if Paul is concerned with establishing the validity of the *same* law which he seems to reject, then it must be the law as a legal entity rather than the law as Scripture.[4]

We may criticize Rhyne's reasoning from another perspective

---

[4]C. Thomas Rhyne, *Faith Establishes the Law*, SBL Dissertation Series 55, Chico: Scholars Press, 1981, pp. 71-74. Rhyne adds that the mention of Scripture in Rom 4:3 further establishes the understanding of *nomos* in 3:31 as Scripture. But the Greek word for Scripture at 4:3 is *graphê* (literally "writing"), not *nomos*. If Paul had wanted to emphasize the similarity between the two texts, why did he switch terms? The presence of *graphê* in 4:3 says nothing about the meaning of *nomos* in 3:31.

as well. According to Rhyne, *nomos* in Romans 3:31 refers to Scripture. The story of Abraham, *drawn from Scripture*, to which Paul refers in Romans 4, is thus intended to demonstrate how Paul upholds Scripture. But, one may ask, does Romans 4 actually provide the reader with an explanation or defense of the validity of Scripture? Does it show that Paul is concerned primarily with the validity of Scripture? In fact, it does not. Rather, Romans 4 continues the discussion of the relationship between boasting and obedience to the law that was summarized in 3:27. Of course, Scripture is used in Romans 4, but only as a means to an end. The point of Romans 4 is not to defend the validity of Scripture itself. Furthermore, in Romans 4 Paul returns to the discussion of the *nomos*. But every time the term *nomos* appears it clearly refers to the law as legal reality rather than to the law as Scripture. In 4:13,14 and 16 it is explicitly contrasted with faith, and in 4:15, the *nomos* is linked with transgression. If 3:31 is intended to assert the validity of the *nomos* as Scripture and thus to stand as a heading for Romans 4, then the consistently negative use of *nomos* in Romans 4 to indicate the law as legal demand appears rather confusing. According to Rhyne and others, Romans 4 was intended to demonstrate the validty of the *nomos* as Scripture; in fact, Romans 4 never ever speaks of the *nomos* as Scripture.

Our only conclusion can be that the understanding of *nomos* in Romans 3:31 as Scripture is untenable .[5]

Within this discussion of the precise meaning of "law" we may have lost sight of our original question in this section: how does v 31 function in its context, as a conclusion to Romans 3 or as a heading for the story about Abraham in Romans 4? Those who see the verse as a heading for Romans 4 necessarily understand

---

[5] Rhyne's contribution to the study of Rom 3:31 can be found in his study of the *mê genoito* ("God forbid!") formula in Arrian's *Discourses of Epictetus*. Based on a comparison with Epictetus, Rhyne attempted to demonstrate that the question in Rom 3:31a, negated by *mê genoito* in 3:31b, necessarily demanded a longer clarification than that given in 3:31c. This clarification was to be found in Rom 4. Even apart from the criticism of Rhyne we have already provided, we are not persuaded by his comparisons with Epictetus; for our counter-arguments, see Thompson, *"We Uphold the Law." A Study of Rom 3,31 and Its Context*, pp. 50-55.

nomos in it to refer to Scripture. If we have shown the inadequacy of such an interpretation of *nomos*, we have at the same time shown the inadequacy of understanding Romans 3:31 as the heading for Romans 4. The only reasonable understanding of *nomos* in 3:31, an understanding derived primarily from the preceding context, is *nomos* as Mosaic law. And this understanding sets the verse clearly as the conclusion to the argument ending in Romans 3.

If Paul affirms his support of the law of Moses as the conclusion to his argument in chap. 3, how are we to understand this support, given his seemingly negative assessment of that same law, especially in 3:27-28? Is there something about the language he uses in the verse, specifically in the terms "overthrow" and "uphold," that might reveal something of his relationship to the law? Especially within the twentieth century, scholars have suggested that in Romans 3:31 Paul draws on technical terms used in rabbinic discussions about the law.

B. "Overthrow" and "Uphold": Technical Terms?

The question before us now is, What kind of language is Paul using in Romans 3:31? More specifically, do "overthrow" and "uphold" form a pair of words that are often used together, so much so that they might be considered a "technical pair," used only in one particular context? It has been suggested, for example, that "overthrow" and "uphold" often appear in contrast with one another in rabbinic discussions of the Torah.[6] If this is the case, then the very terminology that Paul uses in this verse may help answer the question as to the precise meaning of law (*nomos*) in this verse.

But is it really legitimate to speak of this rabbinic background for "overthrow" and "uphold?" Before answering this question,

---

[6]See, for example, the commentaries of C.E.B. Cranfield and Ernst Käsemann. For a more technical discussion of a possible rabbinic background for the language of Rom 3:31, see Richard W. Thompson, "The Alleged Rabbinic Background of Rom 3:31," *Ephemerides Theologicae Lovanienses* 63 (1987) pp. 136-147.

we may take a brief look at the meaning of those terms in themselves.

When Paul asks if he "overthrows" the law, he uses the Greek verb *katargeô*. This verb is composed of three elements: a preposition (*kata*), the negative "*a*" (technically called "privative alpha"), and the verb derived from the Greek word for "work" (*ergon*). The term combines these three elements and possesses a causative nuance meaning "to make something to be of no effect, to render something invalid, useless", or in an extreme sense, "to annihilate" something. In the context of Romans 3:31 *katargeô* really bears a more negative and destructive sense than is captured by the RSV translation, "overthrow," which might give the reader the impression that Paul has merely reduced the law in importance. On the contrary, Paul is being accused of completely abolishing the validity of the Mosaic law, reducing it to nothing. The charge against Paul is that he denies any value to the law whatsoever.

The very severity of the attack on Paul as it is recorded in Romans 3:31a perhaps compelled Paul to use an equally strong term in his defense of himself in 3:31c; he "upholds" the law. Here the Greek word is *histanô* and, like *katargeô* it bears a causative sense: literally, "to make something stand." Far from destroying the validity of the law, Paul's teaching gives the law its true meaning and authority. Not only does he not reduce its significance for the Christian life, but he positively affirms its real value; he makes the law stand.

Do these two Greek verbs reflect technical terms drawn from rabbinic discussions? We must first note that the Hebrew equivalents for *katargeô* and *histanô* are *bṭl* and *qwm*, respectively. As we have stated, some exegetes have proposed that these terms were used by the rabbis in their discussions of the Torah. But when we look at the texts proposed as examples of this use (and they are very few in number) we find that they do not shed any light on Paul's use of "overthrow" and "uphold" in Romans 3:31. The reason for this is that the rabbinic understanding of the Torah was as broad as the various understandings of *nomos* that we have already seen. In other words, even if the rabbis did use terminology similar to Paul's, the terms were used in such a variety of contexts that, in themselves, they tell us nothing of what it is that may be "overthrown" or "upheld." The rabbis could speak of overthrowing or upholding the Torah as Scripture, but they could also use the same words in discussing the legal aspects of the Torah. This means that even if a rabbinic "overthrow/uphold" formula existed (and this has not been proven), this formula in itself would not tell us anything about the content or meaning of "overthrowing" and "upholding" the law.

A further and more probing criticism can be made of the hypothesis of a rabbinic background for Romans 3:31, however. There is insufficient evidence from the first century to enable us to establish the existence of any such "overthrow/uphold" rabbinic formula. In short, we don't know if there was such a formula, and from the texts in which the words do appear (many of them quite late) we can determine nothing which might illuminate the overthrowing or upholding of the law in Romans 3:31. The so-called rabbinic background of Romans 3:31 has not been demonstrated.

Is there nothing, then, that can be said of Paul's terminology in v 31 that might shed some light on how he understands his upholding the law? Rather than searching in the rabbis, we may find a better source for understanding Paul's use of these terms in Paul's own writings. If we investigate *katargeô* and *histanô* elsewhere in Romans and in Paul's other genuine letters, we discover an interesting pattern of usage.

First, Paul uses the verb "to cause to stand" (*histanô*) at Romans 10:3 and 14:4. In both cases the verb is used transitively (i.e., with an object) as in Romans 3:31. In Romans 10:3 Paul states that the Jews were attempting to "establish" their own righteousness and did not "submit" to the righteousness of God (which had been revealed in Christ). In Romans 10:3, then, "establishing" one's own righteousness is set in opposition to "submitting" to God's righteousness. Turning to Romans 14, we see Paul discussing certain Christians in the Roman community who are "weak" in faith, i.e., they are scandalized when other Christians do not follow the prescriptions of Jewish law regarding restrictions on eating certain kinds of food. Paul argues that no one should pass judgment on another (v 3). In v 4 Paul concludes: "Who are you to pass judgment on the servant of another? It is before his own master that he *stands* or falls. And he will be *upheld*, for the Master is able to *make him stand*." Although each of the terms in italics represents the Greek verb *histanô*, we wish to draw attention to the contrast between "stand" and "fall." In Romans 10:3 the Jews' "setting up" their own righteousness was contrasted with their "non-submission" to God's righteousness. In Romans 14:4, a person is "made to stand" so that he or she does not "fall." In both texts, *histanô* occurs with a contrasting verb.

Similarly, in Romans 3:31, *histanô* is used in a situation of contrast; Paul's teaching does not "overthrow" the law, it "upholds" that law. Keeping in mind this data about "uphold" (*histanô*) we now look at Paul's use of "overthrow" (*katargeô*). We find that it, too, often occurs in situations of contrast.

In Romans 4, for example, Paul demonstrates that God's promises must rest on faith rather than on law since Abraham received the original promise based on his faith rather than on his obedience to the law. In v 14, Paul concludes that if it is those who follow the law rather than those who believe who are to be the recipients of God's promise, then "faith is null and the promise is *overthrown*" (*katargeô*; RSV: "is void"). But in v 16, Paul assures his readers that the promise indeed rests on faith (rather than law) and the promise is thereby "guaranteed." The Greek word for "guaranteed" here is *bebaiôs* which means "steadfast, maintaining firmness," or "standing firm." This meaning is related to *histanô*, "to cause to stand." Thus, in Romans 4:14 and 16, *katargeô* is contrasted with a word very similar in meaning to *histanô*

A similar contrast can be found in 2 Corinthians 3. In this passage Paul is comparing the old covenant, which he characterizes as a "dispensation of death" (3:7), with the new covenant, the "dispensation of the Spirit" (3:8). In v 11, Paul contrasts these two covenants. The one is "fading" (literally: being destroyed, *katargeô*) while the other is "permanent." The word translated by the RSV as "permanent" is the Greek verb *menein*, literally, "to remain." The new covenant remains, endures, is permanent; or, using the imagery of Romans 3:31, one could say that the new covenant "stands." Once again, as in Romans 4:14 and 16, *katargeô* is contrasted with a word related in meaning to *histanô*.

Two points may be drawn from this investigation of some of the uses of "overthrow" and "uphold" in Paul.[7] First, they naturally lend themselves to situations of contrast, either to each other or to similar terms. And second, in the texts we have discussed, the issue which provokes the contrasting terminology is precisely the rather broad issue of the relationship between Paul's Jewish past and his Christian present. In Romans 4:14 and 16, the conflict was between the Jewish law and the promise as fulfilled in Christ; in Romans 10:3, between Jewish righteousness and God's righteousness revealed in Christ; in 2 Corinthians 3 between the old covenant and the new.

In Romans 3:31 we find ourselves in a similar situation—a verbal contrast and the conflict between the law of Moses and faith in Jesus Christ. Just as elsewhere Paul had discussed the relationship between the Jewish understanding of God's promise as revealed in the past by using contrasting terms (either *histanô* or *katargeô*, or similar terms), so in Romans 3:31 Paul attempts to express the difficult relationship between the past and present events of justification with contrasting verbs. We may conclude that it is not necessary to resort to any hypothesis about the technical nature of Paul's language in 3:31. The terms in that verse can easily be understood in the broader context of similar statements about the same general problem that Paul makes elsewhere.

This discussion of the terminology of Romans 3:31 has situated that text within the broader context of Paul's thought. The verse has emerged as a general, summarizing statement concerning the relationship between law and faith. But our

---

[7]For a more thorough investigation of the terms in Paul's writings, along with Paul's use of related terminology, see Thompson, "*We Uphold the Law,*" *A Study of Rom 3:31 and Its Context,* pp. 86-124.

knowledge of the precise content of the law that Paul upholds has not been sharpened. We have seen that the understanding of law (*nomos*) as Scripture is untenable. We will now provide some positive indications that when Paul says he upholds the law, he explicitly means the Mosaic law, and all of its legal stipulations.

C. What Is the Law That Paul Upholds?

Throughout Paul's entire discussion of boasting, which eventually culminated in the exclusion of boasting in 3:27, the notion of obedience to the Mosaic law played a crucial role. Paul first focused on a lack of obedience (2:17-23), and then moved to the radical proposition that obedience—or the lack of it—was irrelevant to the question of righteousness: justification is by faith (3:21-26). If Paul seems to be saying that it does not matter whether you obey the law of Moses or not, then the objection that he is abolishing that law seems to be a valid one.

In Romans 3:31 Paul denies this charge, and maintains that he upholds the law. But when he makes this claim, has he perhaps somehow shifted his understanding of that law, so that the law which he claims to uphold is not exactly the same as the law which he is accused of abolishing? Does he limit the "law" that he upholds to include only certain of its moral prescriptions, for example, while ignoring its ceremonial and cultic demands, such as the need for circumcision?

Some scholars have tried to show that Paul reinterprets the law in just this way, so that when in fact he is accused of destroying the *entire* law of Moses, he responds by saying that he upholds it—but he really means that he upholds only *part* of it. Paul was accused of destroying the law, with its ceremonial, dietary and moral demands, so the argument occasionally runs, but he countered the charge by affirming his fidelity to the central demands of the law, i.e. the moral demands. Heikki Räisfänen, for example, suggests that Paul, within his writings, operates with various notions of law, although he was himself unaware of these differences. According to Räisänen, it is only by unconsciously changing the meaning of "law" from a broad notion in 3:31a (the whole Mosaic law) to a more narrow notion in 3:31c (the moral part of the law) that Paul can maintain that he upholds the law.[8] We must decide if this concept of an unconscious shift in Paul's idea of the law in Romans 3:31 is defensible.

First, in a general way we might ask whether or not our contemporary attitude that ceremonial laws and cultic laws are somehow peripheral or secondary to the moral elements of the law is applicable to Paul as a first-century Jew. Such laws might well appear pointless to the twentieth century mind, but were they equally pointless to Paul, even after his encounter with God's justification in Jesus Christ? We need to remind ourselves that for Paul and his contemporaries, the entire law was given by God, and each and every one of its requirements was rooted in the will of God.

Second, Paul himself no doubt thought of the law as a unity, that is, of individual commands collectively expressing God's will. This unity between cultic and moral commandments can be partially seen in the examples of disobedience to the law that Paul refers to in Romans 2:21-22. There Paul accuses the Jews of disobeying the law, and mentions such examples as stealing, adultery and idolatry. He joins together what we might separate into moral elements (stealing and adultery) and cultic elements (idolatry). He then goes on to speak at some length about the value of circumcision (again, a ritual or cultic element), and its relationship to obedience to the entire law (2:25-29). Perhaps Paul did not maintain the same hierarchy of more important and less important laws that prevails today, that sees moral demands as more important than ritual demands.

This does not suggest, however, that for Paul the command to circumcise, for example, was of the same weight as the prohibitions against adultery or murder. Even in his discussion of circumcision, Paul situates it in the context of moral life (it

---

[8]Räisänen, *Paul and the Law*, pp. 23-28.

is accurate to state that he even subordinates circumcision to a position within the moral life). But to demonstrate how the various laws in the Mosaic code relate to one another is different from claiming that some of the laws are no longer valid.[9]

We find no evidence, then, that Paul consciously divided the law into its less important and more important elements, from cultic, ritual commandments to moral demands. Rather, Paul saw the law as a whole, and related the ritual parts to the moral parts. We further suggest that when Paul claims to uphold the law, he means the Mosaic law in its entirety.

At the same time, however, we shall see that Paul does not merely repeat the traditional Jewish understanding of how that law is to be upheld. Had he done this, the accusation of 3:31a would never have been formulated. To be sure, Paul reinterprets the meaning and significance of various aspects of the law (circumcision is a case in point), but we shall see that by the very act of reinterpreting the law (rather than ignoring it), Paul is "upholding the law." His concern encompasses more than the moral elements of the law of Moses.

We have already spoken, for example, about Paul's concern for circumcision. For the Jew, circumcision symbolized a man's entry into the Mosaic covenant, marking him as a recipient of the blessings God imparted to his own people. Paul has argued that the Jewish idea of being especially chosen by God can no longer be maintained; only faith in Christ puts one in any relationship with God. But does this mean that circumcision no longer has any significance whatsoever? Paul thinks that circumcision maintains a value, even after the revelation in Christ. If he didn't believe this, we would be unable to explain his obvious concern to show that circumcision still has a meaning. This concern is evident in the discussion we have already referred to at 2:25-29. Furthermore, in 3:1 Paul explicitly asks about the value of circum-

[9]In other contexts, Paul can completely relativize the meaning of circumcision, e.g. at Gal 5:6, 6:15 or 1 Cor 7:19. But within the letter to the Romans, Paul seems to maintain at least a limited value for the rite of circumcision.

cision, and in 3:2 he indicates that it still has much value. While he does not immediately clarify what that value is, he returns to the topic in Romans 4.

Although we have argued that Romans 3:31 does not introduce Romans 4 as an example of Paul upholding the value of Scripture, we may now point out that in Romans 4:9-12 Paul does indicate one way in which he upholds the Mosaic law, specifically, circumcision. Paul's main concern in the passage is to demonstrate that Abraham received a share in the righteousness of God *before* he was circumcised. For Paul, this can be verified by consulting the biblical accounts in Genesis, chaps. 15 and 17. Paul argues that the significance of this sequence of events in the Genesis stories is that Abraham, having received righteousness in his *uncircumcised* state, can truly be the father of all those people who are *uncircumcised,* namely, the Gentiles. Of course, Abraham was well-known as the forefather of those who were circumcised, i.e., the Jews. Paul accepts this traditional understanding (see 4:1). But having argued that God is equally the God of the circumcised as well as the uncircumcised (3:29-30), Paul now proves that Abraham is equally the father of the circumcised as well as the uncircumcised. In fact, for Paul, Abraham is the father of us all (see Rom 4:16).

Our immediate interest, however, is not Abraham himself. Our concern for the moment focuses on the meaning that Paul attaches to circumcision. In emphasizing what happened to Abraham before he was circumcised, Paul does not conclude that therefore Abraham's circumcision has no meaning or significance. On the contrary, he states explicitly what its significance, after Christ, is. Circumcision is a sign or seal of Abraham's own righteousness that he had by faith (see 4:11).

Commentators often remark on the positive value of circumcision in Romans 4 without, however, connecting it with the upholding of the law in 3:31. But we think a connection between the meaning of circumcision and the specific role of faith is especially interesting. At 3:31, Paul was accused of destroying the law "through faith." The discussion at Romans 4:9-12 demonstrates that it is precisely through faith and the righteousness that comes by faith that circumcision receives its true meaning and value, as a sign of that righteousness. According to Romans 4, then, circumcision receives its true meaning in the context of righteousness by faith. Paul's teaching on righteousness by faith, far from destroying the significance of circumcision, actually upholds it for Abraham and Jewish-Christians.

The reader may have the impression at this point that the most important aspect of Paul's upholding the law concerns circumcision. This is far from the case. We have dwelt on the topic at some length, however, since it is sometimes argued that Paul really had no concern for the ritual or cultic elements of the law, and concerned himself only with its moral precepts. We merely wish to point out that such an understanding of Paul's attitude to the law, at least in the letter to the Romans, does not do justice to the text.

CONCLUSION

The primary concern of Romans 3:27-30 was the exclusion of boasting and the inclusion of the Gentiles within the realm of justification. Transgression, boasting, and feeling of privilege are all related to obedience, and some of the precise examples of a lack of obedience which Paul provides in 2:17-24 concern moral issues, e.g., stealing and adultery. In Romans 3:31 Paul affirms that he upholds the law, and by that he means the entire law, including both its moral and ritual elements. In Romans 4 Paul's teaching has given the circumcision of Abraham (and thereby at least a part of the ritual law) a value within the dispensation of righteousness by faith. But how or where does Paul's teaching uphold the moral law? While not addressing this question immediately in Romans 4, Paul does return to the issue later in the letter, namely at chap. 8, and we investigate his understanding of the law in that section now.

4

How the Law Is Fulfilled in Us
Romans 3:31 and 8:4

In our study of Romans 3:31 we have detemined that the objection raised against Paul in 3:31a is that he set aside the demands of the law of Moses to the point that it seemed as though he taught that the law need not be obeyed, that its precepts and prohibitions were without value. Paul's emphatic denial of the charge consisted in the brief retort that, on the contrary, he upheld the law of Moses. Immediately thereafter, in Romans 4, Paul devoted some attention to one aspect of the Mosaic law, circumcision, and demonstrated how he upheld that rite. But one may legitimately ask if Paul provides a more lengthy exposition of his understanding of how his teaching upholds the law at some other point in the letter to the Romans. Many scholars have suggested that this clarification can be found in Romans 8, specifically in v 4, and we look at that text now in order to see how it might illuminate Paul's own understanding of how he upheld the law of Moses.

Before we discuss the specific content of Romans 8:4, we can point out that it is not unusual for Paul to mention something in passing, only to return to a fuller explanation of it at a later point in his writings. In Romans 3:1, for example, Paul had asked whether the Jews have any advantage in being Jews. While not answering the question immediately, Paul does return to the topic in a general way in Romans 9-11. More specifically, the reference to the possible unfaithfulness of God in Romans 3:3 is expanded at Romans 9:6-9. Likewise, a question raising the possibility of injustice on God's part in Romans 3:5 is answered at Romans 9:14-18. As a final example, we note that the question of whether or not we should sin so that more grace might abound, which first appears in 3:8, is taken up again in 6:1 and 6:15. Thus, for Paul to return to the question of upholding the law in 3:31 at some later point in the letter (e.g., at 8:4) is not inconsistent with his general writing style.[1]

Before turning to the relationship between Romans 3:31 and Romans 8:4, however, we will first determine the meaning of the latter text.[2] Romans 8 is the last of three chapters in which Paul deals with individual issues at some length, namely sin (ch. 6), the law (ch. 7), and the Spirit (ch. 8). In Romans 8:1-11 Paul talks about life in the Spirit. He begins by assuring his readers that they no longer need suffer condemnation because the reign of the Spirit of life in Christ Jesus has set them free from the reign of sin and death.[3] For God has done what the weakness of the law could not do: he has condemned sin in the flesh through the sending of his Son. The purpose of this sending or the result to be achieved by it is expressed in v. 4: "in order that the just requirement of the law might be fulfilled in us, who walk not according to the flesh but according to the Spirit."

One question that must be answered concerns the precise content of the just requirement of the law. Furthermore, we must determine why Paul says it is fulfilled (passive voice) "in us," rather than that we fulfill it, or that it is fulfilled "by

---

[1]For further examples of Paul's technique of resuming earlier questions as topics for discussion, see Hendrikus Boers, "The Problem of Jews and Gentiles in the Macro-Structure of Romans," *Neotestamentica* 15 (1981) 1-11.

[2]For more details, see Richard W. Thompson, "How Is the Law Fulfilled in Us? An Interpretation of Romans 8:4," *Louvain Studies* 11 (1986) 31-40.

[3]The RSV translation, which reads "law" in place of "reign," can mislead the reader into thinking of the Mosaic law or the Pentateuch. Although some scholars have recently defended this interpretation, it is better to see Paul's statements here referring to the rule or reign of death opposed to the rule or reign of the Spirit (see 6:12, 14). For a more thorough exposition, see Thompson, "*We Uphold the Law.*" *A Study of Rom 3,31 and Its Context*, pp. 265-73.

us." Finally, we must discuss the significance of the imagery of "walking" according to the flesh or the Spirit.

A. The Just Requirement of the Law in Romans 8:4

Most commentators agree that when Paul talks about the "just requirement of the law" he is referring to some of the legal requirements of the law of Moses. But which ones in particular? Note that Paul says "requirement" (singular), rather than "requirements." Is he perhaps reducing all the various legal demands to one, and if so, to which one?

Some light can be shed on this problem by comparing Romans 8:4 to Galaltians 5:13-16:[4]

> For you were called to freedom, brethren; only do not use your freedom as an opportunity for the flesh, but through love be servants of one another. For the whole law is fulfilled in one word, 'You shall love your neighbour as yourself.' But if you bite and devour one another take heed that you are not consumed by one another. But I say, walk by the Spirit, and do not gratify the desires of the flesh.

This passage bears some striking similarities with Romans 8:4. First, just as "Spirit" becomes an important notion in the letter to the Romans especially in chap. 8, so in Galatians, "Spirit" occurs most frequently in the verses immediately following 5:13-16. Second, the Spirit/flesh contrast appears for the first time in Romans at 8:4 and then re-occurs four times before 8:14. Similarly, in Galatians the same contrast appears twice before Galatians 5:16, but three times within 5:16-17. Finally, the convergence of other themes and ideas (freedom: Rom 8:2,4; Gal 5:13; fulfillment: 8:4 and 5:14;

---

[4]For the original presentation of this comparison, see H.W.M. van de Sandt, "Research into Rom. 8:4a: the Legal Claim of the Law," *Bijdragen* 37 (1976) 252-69.

walking according to the Spirit: 8:4 and 5:16; and the negative aspects of the flesh: 8:4 and 5:15-16) points to the similarity between these two passages.

One can also find a similarity between Romans 8:2 and Gal 5:13 (Christian freedom from sin) and also between Romans 8:4b and Galatians 5:16 (walking according to the Spirit). These two sets of texts together act as a frame around Romans 8:4a and Galations 5:14:

Romans 8:2	=	Galatians 5:13
Romans 8:4a	=	Galatians 5:14
Romans 8:4b	=	Galatians 5:16

The content of the two middle verses is equivalent: love of neighbor (Gal 5:14) is the fulfillment of the just requirement of the law (Rom 8:4a).

This understanding of the "just requirement" is also confirmed by other texts within Romans itself. In 13:8-10, for example, Paul returns to the theme of law. There he argues that Christians owe no debt except love and that the one who loves his or her neighbor has fulfilled the law (13:8b). Paul then lists specific commandments as possible ways in which the general exhortation to love might be concretized (no adultery, murder, theft) and repeats his conviction that, in fact, all commandments are summed up in love of neighbor (13:9). Quite simply, "Love is the fulfilling of the law" (13:10).

If the just requirement of the law in Romans 8:4 is love of neighbor, a second problem enters the discussion. How is love of neighbor "fulfilled in us?" Paul uses a passive voice (be fulfilled) here. Furthermore, he does not clearly say who it is that does the fulfilling. Rather than say that "we might fulfill the just requirement of the law," Paul writes, "that the just requirement of the law might *be* fulfill*ed in* us." Does Paul really intend to say, "Of course, it is we who fulfill the law," even though he uses a passive voice and the phrase "in us" (not "by us")? Or does Paul remove the ultimate responsibility for our behavior to some higher agency? Does he mean to imply that the law is fulfilled "in us" by someone else? To answer these questions we must examine Paul's argument here more closely.

B. The Significance of the Passive Voice in Romans 8:4

Those who have been raised in a tradition which sees no difficulty in the notion that Christians themselves actively fulfill the law may be surprised to learn that Romans 8:4 is often interpreted to mean that the fulfillment of the law spoken of here is the work of God rather than the accomplishment of individual men and women. Naturally, no one would deny the element of divine grace which activates and energizes a virtuous life, but can Romans 8:4 be used to reject the notion that Christians actually fulfill the law themselves? Does the text really mean that the law is "fulfilled in us" through some agency other than our own decision making and subsequent action? Some commentators suggest that this is indeed the case.

Of course, their motives are honorable. They wish to protect the sovereignty of God in the process of justification, and they hasten to deny that the ultimate responsibility for that justification lies within any person's own power. But the point at issue here really does not concern such theological issues as this. Rather, in the context of the letter to the Romans, the question must focus on what *Paul* meant by announcing that the law "might be fulfilled in us."

Scholars who see Romans 8:4 as affirming the exclusive action of God point to texts as 7:1-6 in support of their interpretation. This text seems to imply that Christians have been freed from the law (see especially 7:1-4). According to this interpretation, to speak then of Christians actually fulfilling the law in Romans 8:4 could be dangerous or misleading.[5] Other scholars explicitly affirm that the fulfillment of the

[5]See Ernst Käsemann, *Commentary on Romans*, Grand Rapids: Eerdmans, 1980, p. 218.

law spoken of in 8:4 refers to the action of God, not to the behavior of men and women.[6] At the other end of the spectrum, we find scholars who affirm just the opposite understanding of Romans 8:4 and boldly translate Paul's Greek passive voice with the English active voice: "that we might fully accomplish" or "that we might do completely." The translation of Romans 8:4 then becomes: "God did this so that we, who live according to the Spirit and not according to human nature, might do completely what the Law demands as just."[7] Thus, we can find interpretations that take the passive voice literally and emphasize the activity of God as well as interpretations that ignore the Greek passive and translate it with an English active voice.

Is either of these conflicting interpretations correct? In order to answer this question, a few points need to be kept in mind. First, the grammatical form of "fulfill" in Paul's Greek text is clearly passive and any English translation of this form should reflect the passive voice; there is no reason to give it an active translation. At the same time, it must be understood that this use of the passive voice need not reflect any assault whatsoever on an active understanding of Christians fulfilling the law. Paul clearly writes "that the requirement of the law *might be fulfilled*," but he is not therefore eager to impress upon his readers the impossibility (or unsuitability) of Christians themselves actually fulfilling the law. On the contrary, this activity on the part of Christians is equally as important as the divine intervention, and is expressed again, for example, at Romans 13:8b.

Already at 8:4 we find an emphasis on the necessity and appropriateness of human activity in fulfilling the law. We can point to four indications of this. First, the preceding context (Rom 7) consistently points to the question of human

[6]See, for example, C.E.B. Cranfield, *A Critical and Exegetical Commentary on the Epistle to the Romans*, 2 vols., International Critical Commentary, Edinburgh: T. and T. Clark, 1975-79, vol. 1, p. 224.

[7]See B.M. Newman and E.A. Nida, *A Translator's Handbook on Paul's Letter to the Romans*, Helps for Translators 14, Stuttgart: United Bible Society, 1973, pp. 147-48.

ability (and inability) to fulfill the law (or do good: see especially 7:15-25). Second, the usual understanding of the Greek word for fulfull (*plêroô*) normally includes specific matters of behavior, points of law to be fulfilled. Third, as we shall see, the conclusion of 8:4 clearly specifies the locus and manner of the fulfilling of the law, both of which center on human activity. And fourth, the verses following 8:4 again illuminate the importance of human behavior (see especially 8:5-8).

To sum up, the voice of the verb "fulfill" in Romans 8:4 is obviously passive and should be so translated. This in no way, however, excludes any notion of real human responsibility in fulfilling the law. In fact, Paul reinforces the concept of human responsibility in the remainder of the verse and in the rest of Romans 8 as well. The passive voice alone, then, does not support a direct attack on Christians' active responsibility in fulfilling the law. As we proceed to the next phrase of the verse, it may appear once again that Paul is hedging on the amount of human responsibility involved by stating that the law is fulfilled "in us" rather than "by us." But what is the real significance of the preposition "in"?

C. "In Us" or "By Us" in Romans 8:4?

Paul uses the expression "in us" (Greek: *en hêmin*) to clarify further the manner of the fulfillment of the law. Two grammatical possibilities exist for the interpretation of this dative prepositional phrase. First, a local sense, which focuses attention on the "locus" or place of the fulfillment, i.e. "in us" or "among us," is possible. Second, the Greek expression "in us" may be taken in an instrumental sense, i.e., "by us" or "through us," with "us" being the agent of the fulfilling of the law.

Those who have interpreted Romans 8:4 as defending the sovereignty of the action of God, exclusive of any ultimate human responsibility, prefer to understand "in us" in the local sense. A parallel instance of such a usage can be seen in

Galatians 2:20: "it is no longer I who live but Christ who lives *in me*".[8] In clear opposition to this approach to "in us" we find other scholars who boldly translate the Greek phrase "by us," thus making explicit the claim that we actually fulfill the law.[9] Still other exegetes think that either interpretation is correct.[10]

Our own interpretation of Romans 8:4 so far has favored the inclusion of human responsibility in the action of fulfilling the law. Why then, we must ask, did Paul not simply write "by us" if that is what he really intended to say? Paul could easily have used the same Greek expression found in Romans 15:24, for example, in which he communicates his hope to see the Romans on his way to Spain, "and to be sped on my journey to Spain *by* you." But rather than take this option Paul used "in us" in 8:4 to preserve the notion of human responsibility without focusing exclusively on the human side of the action. The phrase "in us" can include the meaning "by us," as in a similar text at Romans 1:12. There Paul writes that part of his reason for wanting to go Rome is so that he might be encouraged, literally, "in you," i.e. in the Romans (RSV: "mutually"). To be encouraged "in the Romans" necessarily means "by the Romans" as well as "among" them. Thus the preposition "in" is used here in both an instrumental ("by") and local ("among") sense.

There are reasons for thinking that "in us" at Romans 8:4 also bears an instrumental sense. First, we can find such reasons in the preceding and following contexts of the verse. In Romans 7, for example, the Greek phrase "in me" is frequently found (vv 8, 17, 18, 20; the RSV sometimes translates "within me"). In 7:20 Paul writes: "Now if I do what I do not want, it is no longer I that do it, but sin which

[8]See, for example, Käsemann, *Commentary on Romans*, p. 219.

[9]See Heinrich Schlier, *Der Römerbrief*, Herders theolgischer Kommentar zum Neuen Testament 6, Freiburg: Herder, 1977, p. 243.

[10]See Ulrich Wilckens, *Der Brief an die Römer*, Evangelisch-Katholischer Kommentar zum Neuen Testament 6/1, Zurich: Benziger Verlag and Neukirchen— Vluyn: Neukirchener Verlag, 1978, p. 126 and n. 525.

dwells within me." Although "within me" here is clearly local, the notion of personal responsibility has already been stated in the first part of the verse: "If I do not do what I want." If a person does evil, then, who is responsible, the person or sin? It is clear that the agent does what he does not want to do, and yet at the same time it is not the person who is doing it but sin dwelling in him. It is difficult to see that the question of responsibility or agency lies totally on one side (the person) or the other (sin).

In Romans 8:1-4 Paul has presented the antithesis to the prevailing situation described in Romans 7 (see especially Rom 8:2: "the law of the Spirit of life in Christ Jesus has set me free from the law of sin and death"). The "in us" of 8:4 recalls the "in/within me" of chap. 7. Paul contrasts two ways of living, two modes of existence. Both work and develop "in" persons. Whatever force "sin" may have in influencing a person's actions or whatever effect the Spirit may exert on a person's behavior, the law is nonetheless fulfilled (or not!) "in" us, or "among" us, and necessarily also "by" us.

We conclude that Paul's vocabulary in Romans 8:4 should be respected; the law is fulfilled "in us." But this phrase easily includes active human responsibility in that fulfilling, and we see no polemic against human effort contained in the phrase. In fact, the very addition of "in us" seems to focus precisely on human responsibility. Paul could easily have left the phrase out completely. He could have alleged that "God sent his Son in order that the just requirement of the law might be fulfilled," and left it at that. But by adding the prepositional phrase (and the rest of the verse), Paul specifically draws attention to human behavior. The just requirement of the law is only fulfilled in persons who actually obey the law: the divine aspect of God sending his Son and the human aspect of obedience appear to be equally important.

As if to emphasize the point one last time, Paul further completes Romans 8:4 with an extended participial phrase describing the lives of those who fulfill the law. They are those who walk, not according to the flesh, but according to the Spirit. A few comments are in order.

D. "Who Walk..." in Romans 8:4

Paul describes those who fulfill the law as those "who walk according to the Spirit." The use of "walk" in the NT to indicate a way of life is not uncommon and such usage is often encountered in Paul (see e.g. Rom 13:13; 14:15; Gal 5:16). The "walk" imagery situates us once again in the realm of human behavior. This emphasis in Romans 8:4 is also illuminated when we compare the text with another in the same letter, Romans 6:4.

Shortly before Romans 6:4 Paul reacts to the outrageous notion that one should sin so as to provide more opportunities for the spread of grace (6:1). In refuting this perverse notion Paul draws a parallel between Christ's burial and resurrection and the believer's baptism and daily life. At 6:4 Paul writes: "We were buried therefore with him by baptism into his death, so that as Christ was raised from the dead by the glory of the Father, we too might walk in newness of life."

Let's take a look at the logic of this verse. Both Christ and Christians have been buried, Christ literally in a tomb and Christians figuratively in baptism. After his literal burial Christ was raised from the dead; after their figurative burial Christians should be able to walk in newness of life. Christ's resurrection from the dead after burial is a parallel to Christians walking in newness of life after baptism. Paul can even intensify the logical sequence of events: we were buried with him *in order that* (Greek: *hina*) we might walk in newness of life. Just as Christ rises from burial into resurrection life, so too Christians must rise from baptism into a new manner of daily life.

At Romans 8:4 Paul has again connected the *magnalia Dei* in Christ to the ordinary life of the believer with a text somewhat parallel to 6:4. At 8:4 Paul no longer explicitly speaks about Christ's burial and resurrection, but fixes his gaze on a prior moment, the sending of the Son (which ultimately includes burial and resurrection). But just as the immediate significance of Christ's resurrection is the new life in which the believer should walk, so too the purpose of Christ's coming into the world is specified as Christians being able to walk according to the Spirit. We have seen that, notwithstanding the passive voice of "fulfill" and the somewhat ambiguous "in us," Paul lucidly focuses his attention on the necessity of Christian fulfillment of the law, and specifies where and how that fulfillment takes place.

We can now return to our original question about Romans 8:4; namely, how it can be seen as a further clarification of what Paul means when he says he upholds the law in 3:31.

E. Romans 3:31 and Romans 8:4

In Romans 3:31 Paul answers the objection that by his teaching he makes the law of Moses meaningless. He insists that he upholds the law, and we have seen that by "law" he means the entire law of Moses. Paul returns to the question of fulfilling the law in Romans 8:4. There he speaks of its just requirement, by which he means the command to love one's neighbor. In Romans 8:4 Paul delicately balanced two aspects of obedience, i.e., human behavior and divine grace.

It is clear that both Romans 3:31 and 8:4 refer to obedience to the Mosaic law. But what about the dual notion of human and divine activity? Some exegetes emphatically deny any correlation between 3:31 and 8:4 on the basis that the first text refers exclusively to humans fulfilling the law while the second text refers exclusively to God's activity. We have already seen that this understanding of 8:4 is too narrow. If Paul had wanted to exclude human action from his thought in that text, he should have eliminated the last half of the verse.

It is also possible to see a dual understanding of human activity and divine grace in Romans 3:31 as well as 8:4. First, we can point to the element of faith present in 3:31. Paul's accusers apparently protested that he was destroying the law through his idea of faith. If justification was now by faith, they reasoned, then obedience to the law is no longer necessary nor important. Paul's answer to their charge implies that he upholds the law through faith. His teaching on faith does not eliminate the law from the Christian life (3:31). Further, Paul later shows that his teaching on faith forms a basis for the importance of the law in the Christian life (8:4). The two texts are not equivalent. By upholding the law in 3:31 Paul primarily refers to his teaching whereas the fulfillment in 8:4 (cf. walking according to the Spirit) points to moral behavior. But in both passages the human and divine aspects of obedience to the law are present:

Divine Element	*Human Element*
3:31 through faith (in Christ)	*we* uphold the law
8:4: be fulfilled (passive)	in *us* who walk ...

We cannot agree with scholars who see a sharp distinction between these two passages whereby 3:31 speaks exclusively about humanity while 8:4 speaks exclusively about God. In fact, both texts speak of a union of human and divine action with reference to the Mosaic law.

CONCLUSION

In Romans 3:31 Paul had announced a topic to which he would return later in his letter to the Romans. The objection about overthrowing the law and the need for his defense that he upholds the law were brought on by his teaching on faith and its implications for the Jews. In Rom 8:4 Paul implies that the fulfillment of the law has to do with human behavior. In Rom 13:8-10, this point is made explicit: love is the fulfilling of the law.

But if justification is by faith, and God justifies everyone on the same basis, then what becomes of Jewish identity and Jewish law? In 3:31 the objection about the law is formulated, and quickly dismissed (it will be taken up later). In Romans 4 Paul begins to talk about Abraham. We have already shown that Romans 4 is not an explanation of how Paul upholds Scripture (as some had interpreted 3:31). But why does Paul talk about Abraham after 3:27-31, and how does Romans 4 fit into the general context of universal justification that has been established especially since 3:27? A closer look at Romans 4 is now in order.

5

Abraham, the Father of Us All
Romans 4

Paul's discussion of Abraham in Romans 4 follows immediately upon his statement that he upholds the law in 3:31. We have already argued that chap. 4 does not form a scriptural clarification of 3:31 understood as a statement about Scripture. There is even a certain tension between the statement in 3:31 and the beginning of 4:1, "What then shall we say?" With this formula, which he uses elsewhere in his letter to the Romans, Paul is beginning a new phase in his argumentation, a phase still related of course to what precedes, but at the same time moving to a new aspect of the matter under discussion. It seems clear that in 4:1, while Paul has not abandoned his concerns about the exclusion of boasting in 3:27 and the universal act of justification for Jew and non-Jew alike in 3:28-30, he has moved nonetheless to a new level in his argument. We will examine this new element in Paul's thought, the relationship between his teaching and the Jewish understanding of Abraham, from the three central points that have emerged in 3:27-30: the exclusion of boasting, the universality of justification in Christ, and the element of faith.

A. Abraham and the Exclusion of Boasting

We know that in 3:27-30 Paul makes explicit his claim
that justification by faith necessarily means that all humanity
is related to God in Christ on an equal basis. Fulfilling the
law or performing "works" is no longer the basis on which
one is related to God. In 3:31 Paul briefly refutes the criticism
that his understanding of faith nullifies the law. In 4:1, he
turns to Abraham.

Apparently, Paul found it necessary to introduce the patriarch into the discussion at this point. What is the Jewish
understanding of Abraham that compelled Paul to discuss
him here? A clue is given already in 4:1, in which Paul
designates Abraham as "our forefather according to the
flesh"[1] Paul is drawing on a traditional Jewish understanding
of Abraham as the father of all the circumcised, i.e., those
who are Jews "according to the flesh" (remember that Paul
had employed the same technique of using traditional Jewish
ideas in his argumentation at 3:30). Essentially, at 4:1 Paul is
asking what a proper understanding of Abraham can be if,
in fact, being a Jew according to the flesh is now irrelevant in
the matter of justification. Does Abraham, as the father of
the Jews, also become irrelevant?

But Paul moves to a discussion about Abraham in Romans
4 for another reason as well, and that is the connection
between the exclusion of boasting and the performance of
works.[2] Earlier Paul had argued that the Jews could not
boast in their works because they did not possess sufficient
works; they did not obey the law. But in the popular mind of
Paul's day Abraham was understood to be one person who
in reality had actually obeyed the law. Abraham did have

---

[1]The Greek text of Rom 4:1 is uncertain. For a translation that departs from the
RSV rendering, see Richard B. Hays, "'Have We Found Abraham to Be Our
Forefather According to the Flesh?' A Reconsideration of Rom. 4:1," *Novum
Testamentum* 27 (1985) 76-98.

[2]For a more technical treatment of the question of Abraham and his relationship
with boasting, see Jan Lambrecht, "Why is Boasting Excluded? A Note on Rom
3,27 and 4,2," *Ephemerides Theologicae Lovanienses* 61 (1985) 365-69.

works. And if he did, perhaps this means that Abraham can boast. And if Abraham can boast, then, contrary to Paul, boasting has not been excluded.

Paul answers this question about Abraham in Romans 4:2: "For (a) if Abraham had been justified by works, (b) he has something to boast about, (c) but not before God." In order to understand the very compact reasoning process Paul follows in this verse, it is necessary to divide it into three parts, as we have done. First, regarding v 2a (the protasis, the "if" clause), we must ask whether or not Paul means to imply that Abraham was in fact justified by his works. On a purely grammatical level, this is a possible, though not probable, interpretation of the Greek text. But the reader is not intended to understand the text in this way. It would be very surprising indeed, after the long argument about the Jews' failure to obey the law in 2:17-3:30, and after the exclusive emphasis on faith rather than works as operative in justification in 3:27-31, that now Paul would admit that Abraham was an exception to this universal dispensation of faith. The preceding context of Romans 4:2 demands that we understand it as posing a condition contrary to fact: what *if* Abraham *had been* justified by his works (of course, we know that he wasn't)?

The apodosis (v 2b, the "then" clause), which follows the protasis (v 2a), seems to contradict his whole teaching about faith as the basis for justification. For in 4:2b Paul says that (if Abraham had been justified by works) then yes, he has something to boast about. We must admit that there in v 2b Paul is suddenly reasoning on a purely theoretical level. If Abraham is justified by works (in fact, he wasn't), then he has a right to boast.

In v 2c Paul further complicates the matter by placing a qualification on Abraham's right to boast in 2b: "but not before God." Many exegetes are tempted to expand this part of the verse to mean that Abraham had a reason to boast before himself and before others, but he had no reason to boast before God. But is this correct? Does Paul actually permit a certain compromise here with his previous position that no Jew can boast by making an exception for Abraham?

In v 2b there is probably no limitation with regard to Abraham's right to boast and, thus, no qualification is placed on it. Paul is speaking theoretically, and in the realm of theory he can grant that if there are good works, then there may be legitimate boasting. But a shift occurs in v 2c, and here Paul returns from the speculative world of theory back to the concrete world of reality. When he explicity states "but not before God" Paul is no longer thinking of a hypothetical boasting based on hypothetical works. In v 2c Paul is returning to the realm of the real world, and to the action of God in Christ which has concretely occurred in history.

In v 2b, Paul grants the possibility that, with works, Abraham could boast. But suddenly, in v 2c, Paul realizes that, in fact, this theoretical situation never occurred at all. Abraham, too, was justified by faith. In the real world of how God actually deals with all persons—including Abraham— there can be no boasting. One could only boast in the fantasy world of "what if." In the world of the action of God in Christ (see 3:21-26), no one can boast. This is the meaning of "but not before God." In the realm of reality, the realm of God, there can be no boasting.

God justified Abraham simply because of his faith, not because of his works. This idea is clearly stated in v 3, which explains v 2 by means of a Scripture quotation: "For what does the scripture say? 'Abraham believed God, and it was reckoned to him as righteousness.'" This is the very reason that boasting is excluded, because in fact Abraham received righteousness as a gift, in faith, and not through works.

Furthermore, in vv 4-5 the two alternatives—righteousness through works or righteousness through faith—are once again placed in opposition to one another, although in different terminology. In v 4, Paul presents the situation of a person who receives righteousness through works; for this person, righteousness would be considered something that the person had earned and therefore had a right to. In v 5, Paul provides the alternative view. The one who does not work but who believes God, this one is made righteous freely, by way of a gift. It is important to remember, however, that the first alternative (v 4) never became a reality. Even with Abraham, we do not have an example of someone who received righteousness through works. The second alternative (v 5) in fact describes not only the situation of Abraham, but the possibility that remains open for all who have faith, both Jews and Gentiles alike.

When we discussed Romans 3:27 in Chapter One we saw that it contained a summary of Paul's first argument that boasting is eliminated because there were no works on which to base the boast (2:17-3:20) and his second argument that, in any case, justification is by faith in Christ (3:21-26). We stated that in v 27 the "No" to the question as to whether boasting is excluded by the law of works may surprise the reader of 2:17-3:20. The reader rather expects a "Yes" which is then explained as follows: Yes, boasting is excluded by the law of works, since as a matter of fact, these works do not exist; boasting is thus excluded by their absence. Everybody, including the Jew, is a sinner!

In the Additional Note (see pp. 29-30) we presented an alternative understanding of this "No" which argues as follows. Boasting is not excluded by the works of law. If they exist, then boasting is permitted. In our discussion of 4:2, we find a similar logical connection applied to Abraham. Yet, the protasis (the if-clause) here in v 2 is contrary to fact: "If Abraham *had been* justified by works (but he was not!)."

Paul has brought together a renewed understanding of Abraham and his teaching on boasting. But he has not finished with the venerable patriarch just yet. Paul resolutely pushes his conclusions still further, justification in Christ is for Jew and non-Jew alike. And Abraham himself takes his place in this new dispensation of grace, for he is truly the father of all—Jew and non-Jew alike.

B. Abraham and the Universality of Justification

In our previous discussion of how Paul upholds the law,

we noted that he has given a new significance to the Jewish rite of circumcision in the dispensation of faith. Abraham received circumcision as a sign or seal of the righteousness that he had by faith even before he was circumcised (4:11). In that earlier discussion, we pointed out that circumcision was not Paul's primary concern. Now we can look at the broader context in which this discussion of circumcision is placed, and see the more profound meaning of circumcision in Paul's theology of universal justification.

In 4:11, after explaining what the significance of circumcision is, Paul then tells the reader why it is that Abraham received righteousness by faith in his uncircumcised state: "The purpose was to make him the father of all who believe without being circumcised but also follow the example of the faith which our father Abraham had before he was circumcised." Abraham was made righteous before he was circumcised, Paul argues, so that he might legitimately be the father of those who are now made righteous without being circumcised. Not only does God justify the circumcised and the uncircumcised alike on the same basis, but Abraham is indeed also the father of all who are justified on that basis, whether in a state of circumcision or not. Abraham is the father of Jews (circumcised) and Gentiles (uncircumcised) alike.

To affirm Abraham as the forefather of the Jews is to affirm a special relationship that the Jews have with God. But Paul next returns to one of his favorite themes, namely, that the law does not give one any special privilege with regard to God. In 4:13-15, Paul raises the question of the law, now in relation to God's promise to Abraham. To understand these verses, we need some background from the Hebrew Scriptures.

In the story of Abraham recounted in Genesis 15, God makes two promises to Abraham. The first is that Abraham will have numerous descendants, as many as the stars in the heavens (Gen 15:5). Abraham believes this promise of God, and his faith is "reckoned to him as righteousness" (15:6). A second promise is then made to Abraham, that he and his descendants will inherit a land (15:7). This second promise is confirmed in a covenant between God and Abraham (15:17-21). In Romans 4, Paul speaks about both of these promises. In 4:13-16, he comments on the promise of the land; starting in v 17, he takes up the promise of the descendants.

Paul is eager to demonstrate that the promise of the land did not come to Abraham because he obeyed the law (4:13). If this had been the case, then Abraham would be a model for others to obey the law and thus receive the promise of the land. But this would mean that faith has no role to play at all—the promise could be gained by obedience. Furthermore, the promise itself would lose its specific character as "promise." If it could be earned by obeying the law (4:14), if it necessarily must be given to those who are obedient, in what sense would it really be a "promise," something originating in a relationship of trust rather than merit?

But the deeper reason that the promise is given to those who have faith rather than to those who obey the law is so that the promise can rest on the gracious action of God. If the promise could be earned, then those who earned it would receive it automatically. But if it rests on faith, according to Paul, then it rests on the grace of God (4:16a). And for Paul this basis on the gracious action of God has a very important practical consequence. It is only in this way that the promise can be guaranteed to *all* of Abraham's descendants, not only to the Jews who possess the law, but likewise to those who share in the faith of Abraham, i.e., the Gentiles (4:16b). In this way the integrity of the promise—as promise—is safeguarded. God's gracious plan to justify the whole world can endure and Abraham can be revered as the father of us all (4:16c).

In one quick stroke Paul recalls his designation of Abraham at the beginning of Romans 4 as "our forefather according to the flesh." Nowhere has Paul denied the value of Abraham as the father of the Jews who believe in Christ, but he equally affirms Abraham as the father of non-Jews as well. Abraham is father, therefore, no longer simply "according to the flesh", but now "in the presence of God" (4:17). The limits of Abraham's humanity as a circumcised man are transcended in God's plan, so that, from the perspective of God, he might be the father of all.

C. Abraham's Unwavering Faith

In 4:17 Paul shifts from the promise of the land (which had sparked his discussion in 4:13-16) to the promise that Abraham will be the father of many nations (see 4:18). Paul first situates this discussion in a traditional Jewish context by affirming two typically Jewish understandings of God. He is the God who gives life to the dead and calls into existence things that do not yet exist (4:17). Paul then focuses on Abraham's faith (especially vv 19-22). Two remarks are in order here.

First, how are we to understand the relationship between Abraham's faith and the promise of universal fatherhood? In the Greek text of v 18, Paul claims that Abraham believed, hope against hope, *in order to* become the father of many nations. This means that the purpose of Abraham's believing was to become such a father. The RSV translation gives a weakened sense to this passage. In that version, Abraham's fatherhood is merely the consequence of his faith, not the purpose of it.

Second, one should notice that in Romans 4:1-12 and 4:13-16, Paul has emphasized the gift character of the promise. The promise has come through grace, not through observance of the law. This tension between grace and obedience is consistent with Paul's reasoning throughout these opening chapters of Romans, starting at 2:17. But in 4:17b-21, we have the impression that Paul is speaking in a slightly different tone. Now it is stressed that Abraham "in hope believed against hope that he should become the father of many nations" (v 18), that Abraham did not weaken in faith although he realized that his own body and Sarah's womb were as good as dead (v 19), that he did not doubt God's promise but, on the contrary, grew strong in faith (see v 20ab), that he gave praise to God (v 20c), and remained convinced that God was able to do what he had promised (see v 21). Throughout these verses Paul is stressing again and again, Abraham's personal, active involvement, his steadfastness, his faithfulness. Are we justified in reading v 22 as talking about a reward? "*That is why* his faith was 'reckoned to him as righteousness'"—because of its endurance, its intractability. Could Abraham "boast"—now, not because of works—but because of such impressive faith?

Paul has certainly not raised this question, and no doubt, would answer it with a resounding, "No!" Surely Paul does not present Abraham's faith as a means of "earning" the promise. No one would claim that Paul consciously intended any such idea. But is the emphasis on Abraham's faith here a merely accidental way of speaking? Or is it perhaps more spontaneous, originating in Paul's unreflected but real awareness of the intimate relationship between God's grace and a person's response. If so, then is not this emphasis on Abraham's own faith a remarkable indication that even for Paul, one can overemphasize the fact that justification is only by faith and not by works? In the case of Abraham, Paul tells us a great deal about the quality of Abraham's faith. Does this show us that even for Paul, who denied that obedience could curry favor with God, the quality of an individual's faith is nonetheless of some consequence in the process of justification?[3]

Paul concludes the chapter by focusing on his present readers. Abraham believed and it was reckoned to him as righteousness. But this was not written only for his sake, "but for ours also" (4:24). Paul leads his Christian readers to think of themselves. In 4:24-25, Abraham and the Christians are shown to be parallel in their analogous faith. Just as Abraham believed in a God who was able to bring life (Isaac) from what seemed to be dead, so Christians believe in

[3]Concerning this reflection, and the whole of Chapter Five, see Jan Lambrecht, "'Abraham, notre père à tous.' La figure d'Abraham dans les écrits pauliniens," in P.M. Bogaert (ed.), *Abraham dans la Bible et dans la tradition juive*. Publications de l'Institutum Iudaicum 2, Brussels: Rue des Bollandistes 40, 1977, pp. 118-63.

a God who has raised their Lord, Jesus Christ, from the dead. Amazingly, Paul draws no attention whatsoever to the profound difference between the two who are brought to life, Isaac (who is not even named) and Jesus. It is faith that is important here; it is faith that directly links Abraham and all Christians; it is faith that empowers Abraham to be the "father of us all."

CONCLUSION

With this exposition of the significance of Abraham for Christians Paul brings his teaching on the exclusion of boasting to a close. Boasting in privileged status before God has definitely been excluded—chapters two and three of Romans argued this extensively. At the end of Romans 3, Paul noted, however, that his teaching on the universality of justification did not annul the meaning or significance of the Mosaic Law. In Romans 4 Paul argues that the great patriarch of the Jews, Abraham, also retains a lasting significance in the realm of righteousness. But the significance of the patriarch, as well as that of the law, lies in their relation to faith. And this necessarily means in their relation to Jesus Christ. For God's righteousness has now been revealed, apart from everything else, only in him.

Concluding Reflections
What, Then, Becomes of Boasting?

"What, then, becomes of boasting?" In the end is our beginning, and the question with which we began this study of one section of Paul's writings can challenge us once again. Of course, the terms of the challenge are now different. We are not the faithful Jews of the Mosaic Covenant, relying on the law, and thereby making a special claim on God. We are not those who deny the universal love of God for all men and women, whatever their racial or ethnic origins. We do not insist on circumcision, nor on a physical descent from Abraham. We gladly affirm, with Paul, that Abraham is indeed the father of us all.

In what, then, do we boast? How can this question of nearly two-thousand years ago possibly apply to us? With open minds and hearts, we have conscientiously followed every step of Paul's argument. We have agreed at every turn, nodding in reflective assent along every step of the way. We proudly profess that, in Christ, God is indeed reconciling the entire world to himself (cf. 2 Cor. 5:18-19). We could say, "Yes, Paul, we agree with you!" We have learned your lessons well. Like you yourself, when we boast, we boast in the Lord (1 Cor 1:31).

But it is precisely here that Paul might question the real nature of our boast. When we boast in the Lord, he might ask, are we really focusing our attention on the Lord, or do we sometimes manage to turn the spotlight on ourselves? More specifically, have we learned some of the lessons that might reasonably be drawn from the concluding verses of Romans 3? We can discuss these under the rubrics of the gracious, salvific action of God in Christ, the universality of God's love, and our God-given ability to fulfill the law. In each of these areas, a sinful boasting, akin to that against which Paul railed in Romans, is an ever-present possibility. We can spell this out in more detail.

A. The Gracious Action of God

For Paul, Jewish boasting was excluded for one fundamental reason: in the final analysis, everything is grace. We have been justified freely, in the cross of Christ. We haven't earned it, and we haven't even deserved it. According to Paul, God has demonstrated his love for us in that, while we were still sinners, Christ died for us (Rom 5:8)

However privileged we may feel to have been blessed with this redemption, to have shared in this life through faith, we can in no way succumb to the temptation to think that, if the truth be told, God is really quite lucky to have us on his side. We may pay lip service to the notion that we are sinners, but do we really believe it? When Paul has finally said that it was not because of obedience to the law that the Jews were justified, do we realize that Paul might equally be reminding us that it is not because of our virtue that we are justified? Don't we occasionally feel that it might be more accurate to say that this aspect of Paul's thought really better applies to someone else, certainly not to us?

After all, we're good, decent people. Our lives are directed to serving others, more or less. We aren't flagrant sinners. Surely, God doesn't completely ignore all the natural goodness we share as individual men and women. Surely we have *something* to offer in the negotiations over our ultimate destiny, some small bargaining chip of self-worth that helps to tip the scales of God's justice in our favor.

Paul's Jewish audience had the law of Moses as their ace in the hole. We make no such explicit claims as that. But we nevertheless spontaneously believe in our own goodness, and we may experience considerable discomfort in really accepting Paul's claim that, in fact, God includes us within the ambit of his justifying love by pure grace, freely,—not because of who *we* are, but because of who *God* is.

This extreme focus on the absolute priority of God's grace as that which facilitates our ability to live for him and for others need not be seen negatively, however. To receive this grace, to receive the whole world—not only the macrocosm of the universe but also the microcosm of family, friends, and individual talents—as pure gift, can enable us to see ourselves, in turn, as gift to that same world. To pray with St. Ignatius, for example, that all we have and possess, including our justification, has been given to us by God, is to acknowledge that we, too, are part of that "giveness." We, too, are gift—and gift from God.

For once we have accepted that everything is given by grace, we must further accept that we, too, are part of what is given to the world for its salvation. For Paul, not only have we been *justified* in Christ, but we also now *live* in Christ. We have become part of that gracious cycle of reconciliation, having first received it, but only in order to perpetuate it, to actualize it further in our individual lives. Paul says we are baptized into the death of Christ; in this we are "receivers." But we have been so baptized in order to walk in newness of life, and in this we are "givers."

Our awareness that our ability to live fully human lives has been given us by God's justifying action in Jesus Christ prevents us from boasting in our self-worth, just as it prevented the Jews from boasting in the law. But it need not leave us with a sense of defeat or a fatalistic belief in the depravity of humanity. On the contrary, we accept that we have been graced, in order that we might be bearers of that same grace, in Christ, to the world.

For Paul, God's revelation in Christ was of a universal scope. God is equally the God of all. To share in the process of this revelation as Christians is to share in that universal scope. There is a necessary sense of universal mission inherent in Christianity. And this brings us to the second lesson we can learn from our text in Romans.

B. The Universal Love of God

Especially in Romans 3:27-30, Paul fought against Jewish particularism, the idea that God's promises were made only to a particular group of people, and under particular conditions. We Christians live with the burden of a different kind of particularism, what is sometimes called the "scandal of particularity," that in the one particular man—Jesus—something of universal significance has been achieved.

But we must not let this scandal of particularity and our absolute faith in the salvific meaning of Christ entrap us into a crippling particularism with respect to God's love. For Paul, Jesus Christ was an ultimate, universalizing agent between God and humanity. In Christ, God was not involving himself in what could become simply a new particularism, Christianity instead of Judaism. In Christ, God was reaching out to the entire world, and the entire world, as Paul knew it, was either Jew or Gentile. To argue that God was indeed the God of the Gentiles was to argue for God's universal claim to love the whole world.

Jesus Christ, then, is the one who brings the world together within the realm of God's love. Sometimes, our faith in Christ seems to cause us to narrow our perspective on the love of God rather than broaden it. We see those who are united to Christ as those who are justified; the corollary is that those who are not united to Christ are not justified. But this is to view the world from the wrong perspective.

Paul's encounter with Christ forced him to look at God, and he then discovered a God who was the God of everyone. Our own encounter with Christ, if we take our cue from Paul, must work the same way. Our *Christ*ology must influence our *theo*logy. To know Christ is to know that God loves the whole world.

It sometimes happens that one's vision is slightly distorted here. Paul tries to get us to see Christ as the one who reveals the universal love of God. But when we look at Christ, rather than seeing a broader vision of God, we sometimes see only a narrow vision of Christianity, without which no one can be justified. It is as if we turned a telescope around the wrong way. Rather than using it correctly, so that through the focal point of Christ we see the breadth and depth of God's care for humanity, we look into the wrong end and see the world narrowing to one single point, to a new particularism. But this time, the particularists are Christians instead of Jews.

Paul's understanding of Christianity is that it offers a universal vision of God's love for the whole world revealed in Jesus Christ. We who accept this understanding must at the same time accept the inherent universal mission of Christianity to the world. But the purpose of this mission is not simply to make "converts." Its more profound goal is to enable all peoples and all cultures to share in God's love for them as it is revealed in Christ.

It is possible to view Christianity as a divisive element in the world, providing lines of demarcation between those who are justified and those who are not. This is a flawed vision, one which views everything from the wrong end. Christianity must be seen as a unitive element among peoples, for in Christ, everyone—all peoples—can come to know God's love for them.

C. Fulfilling the Law

The charge against Paul in Romans 3:31 that the law is no longer in effect is still somewhat attractive and often appears to be well-founded. If everything is given by grace, then what difference can it make how we actually live our lives? If I am justified by grace, then how I act doesn't really matter, does it? Such facile reasoning provides us with a soothing balm with which to salve our sometimes troubled consciences.

And yet the very same Paul who argued that everything *is* by grace also argued for the most radically demanding style of life for his Christian communities. We are to put off jealousy, envy, gossiping, backbiting, and all manner of sinful living. Why?

Paul answers that we live in this way, not so that we *can be* justified, but rather precisely because we *have been* justified. God sent his Son into the world for this very purpose (remember Rom 8:4); we are justified by grace so that we might live by grace, so that we might live, in the most profound sense, graciously.

To use Paul's terminology, walking according to the Spirit is not the means whereby we have earned our justification. It is rather a second order of activity; it is a *response* to a prior moment of being justified. To first know that one's life is founded on an initial act of God's grace, and then to accept one's own life as thus "given," further means that one sees all the various activities of an individual life as derived from this initial moment of grace.

How can we claim to have known the God of universal love—in a personal sense, to have been created by this same God as a new creature in Christ—without necessarily affirming this fundamental and personal orientation in our own specific choices, intentions, decisions and movements? To claim that the lives we live are lives of grace is not to say that we are saints. It is simply to record a fact. And if we accept this fact, then we must at the same time admit that the only way we can fully live these already graced lives is by living them in the Spirit. We conform our actions, our concerns, our priorities, to the Spirit of peace, gentleness, patience, and kindness.

We may live according to these norms sometimes out of fear for our future Judge and also in order to gain a reward. But in the first place, we live this way because of who we are. Earlier we noted that God justifies us freely in Christ, not because of what *we* have done nor because of who *we* are, but because of who *God* is. Likewise, we live according to the Spirit primarily because of who we, in Christ, have become, because of who we now are. In this sense, then, we uphold the law—not as a means whereby we earn God's favor, but as a means of specifying our daily lives as lived in the grace we have received.

To this basic, heartening insight, a threefold note must be added. First, "upholding" the law now takes on a moral sense. Paul thought primarily of upholding the law by his teaching, although this of course included a view toward Christian behavior. Second, for Paul, justification is not yet the final salvation. We can never presume to have "done enough" so that we need no longer live by grace. And third, Christians who must live lives of grace by way of a response to God's freely given justification at the beginning, should not forget the future judgement of the same God at the end.

CONCLUSION

"What, then, becomes of boasting?" We have no reason to boast, and we have every reason to boast. We cannot claim privilege because of our innate self-worth, nor because of our virtuous lives. But, like Paul, we can boast in the Lord. For the Lord has justified us in grace, has shared his love with us throughout all ages, and has empowered us to live out our fully human lives in response to him. In this possibility, in this reality in which we move from day to day, and in this Lord, we can boast.

Suggested Readings

Suggested Readings

PAUL IN GENERAL

Neal Flanagan, *Friend Paul. His Letters, Theology and Humanity,* Wilmington: Michael Glazier, 1986. A readable and easy-to-understand introduction to each of Paul's letters that clearly summarizes the major concerns of the text and its interpretation.

John Ziesler, *Pauline Christianity,* Oxford: New York, 1983. A brief and very concise thematic introduction to Pauline theology, presenting the major ideas of Paul's thought, including the place of Christ, the Church, Baptism and Eucharist, and the Jewish law.

THE LETTER TO THE ROMANS

C.E.B. Cranfield, *A Critical and Exegetical Commentary on the Epistle to the Romans,* 2 vol., International Critical Commentary, Edinburgh: T. and T. Clark, 1975-79. An excellent, detailed commentary on the Greek text of the letter to the Romans (also available in an abridged version for the general reader, with the Greek omitted: *Romans. A Shorter Commentary.* Grand Rapids: Eerdmans, 1985).

Brendan Byrne, *Reckoning with Romans. A Contemporary Reading of Paul's Gospel,* Good News Studies 18, Wilmington, Delaware: Michael Glazier, 1986. A non-technical study of the entire letter to the Romans from the perspective of the saving justice of God.

PAUL AND JUDAISM

Ed P. Sanders, *Paul and Palestinian Judaism. A Comparison of Patterns of Religion*, London: SCM Press, 1977. An attempt to understand Palestinian Judaism on its own terms and then to compare it with Paul's thought.

Heikki Räisänen, *Paul and the Law*, Wissenschaftliche Untersuchungen zum Neuen Testament 29, Tübingen: J.C.B. Mohr, 1983. A bold discussion of Paul's teaching on the law and the allegedly inherent contradictions in that teaching.

Ed P. Sanders, *Paul, the Law, and the Jewish People*, Philadelphia: Fortress Press, 1983. A refinement of certain aspects of his *Paul and Palestinian Judaism*, dealing more specifically with the question of Paul's relationship with the Jewish law.

James D.G. Dunn, "The New Perspective on Paul," *Bulletin of the John Rylands Library* 65 (1982-83) 95-122. A development of the discussion initiated by Sanders (see above), with specific attention directed to Paul's understanding of "works of law."

Heikki Räisänen, "Galatians 2.16 and Paul's Break with Judaism." *New Testament Studies* 31 (1985) 543-53. A critical response to Dunn on the meaning of "works of law."

R.H. Gundry, "Grace, Works, and Staying Saved in Paul," *Biblica* 66 (1985) 1-38. A rejection of Sanders' understanding of Judaism and Paul's criticism of it.

_____ *Notes* _____

Notes